🛈 Tourist information	✋ Admission charges:
❓ Other practical information	Very expensive (over $50),
▷ Further information	Expensive ($21–$50),
	Moderate ($7–$20) and
	Inexpensive (under $7)

Introducing Las Vegas

 Las Vegas is the entertainment capital of the world, where sleep is a mere inconvenience interrupting a continuous stream of fun, and where everything is bigger, louder, flashier and trashier than anywhere else in the world.

From the moment you cruise into town it will strike you that this is like no other place. The scale of everything is overwhelming, and The Strip (Las Vegas Boulevard South) in all its blazing glory is a thing of wonderment. Where else can you capture a skyscape that includes the Eiffel Tower, St. Mark's Campanile, an Egyptian pyramid and the Statue of Liberty on the same street? Prepare yourself for a fantasy world made real, where volcanoes erupt and Roman statues come alive.

Evolving from the early saloons, the first casinos and hotels were built in the Downtown area in the 1930s, followed by the expansion of The Strip in the 1940s. Since the late 1980s, mega-hotels have emerged—combining casinos, shopping malls, restaurants, spas and theaters—to offer the complete experience for gamers and vacationers alike. So what continues to bring millions of visitors here annually—gambling millions of dollars in the process? Las Vegas is an ever-evolving metropolis with a restless spirit that is part of its eclectic appeal. Hotels are regularly torn down to make way for brand-new ideas, and entertainment programs constantly change. Vegas is now home to some of the top restaurants in the world, many run by celebrity chefs, and most of the big names in designer fashion have made their mark on the shopping scene.

You might be forgiven for believing Las Vegas is not synonymous with culture and outdoor adventure, but beyond the neon there are some great museums and galleries, and ballet, jazz, symphony orchestras and opera blend perfectly. Away from the urban wonders are dramatic canyons, dams and sparkling lakes, and the terrain lends itself to some of the finest golf courses. But no matter how you spend your time here, this crazy city will never let you forget that the driving force is gambling.

FACTS AND FIGURES

- There are more than 15,000 miles (24,100km) of neon tubing in The Strip and Downtown Las Vegas.
- There are around 500 weddings per day in Vegas.
- There are around 200,000 slot machines to take your cash.
- On average, each visitor to Las Vegas spends US$540 on gambling.

RAT PACK MEETS VEGAS

In the 1960s, Las Vegas was dominated by a group of singing and acting stars. Frank Sinatra first performed at the Sands Hotel in 1960, with John F. Kennedy in the audience. Thereafter, Sinatra, along with Dean Martin, Sammy Davis Jr., Peter Lawford and Joey Bishop—collectively known as the Rat Pack—dominated the scene and drew in huge crowds.

Fodor's
25 Best

LAS VEGAS

Contents

KEY TO SYMBOLS

- ✚ Map reference to the accompanying pull-out map
- ✉ Address
- ☎ Telephone number
- 🕐 Opening/closing times
- 🍴 Restaurant or café
- Ⓜ Nearest monorail station
- 🚌 Nearest bus route
- ♿ Facilities for visitors with disabilities

TYING THE KNOT IN STYLE

Thousands of people are following in the footsteps of the rich and famous and saying "I do" in Vegas. Famous couples such as Elvis and Priscilla Presley, and Bruce Willis and Demi Moore, have been joined by Mr. and Mrs. Average from countries as far apart as Britain and Japan, to get married in some of the 50 or so wedding chapels (▷ 60–61).

HOW IT BEGAN

Spawned from a trading post along the old Spanish Trail, Las Vegas became a popular stop for its freshwater spring. The prospect of gold added to the lure and later the building of the Hoover Dam secured the city's future. The liberal state laws of Nevada allowed the growth of the casinos, and soon the little campsite in the desert developed into a city.

Focus on Playing the Game

Whether you're hoping to hit the jackpot on the high-stakes tables, or just fancy a taste of the slots, it's worth finding out first what the main games are and picking up a few tips along the way.

The Games

Baccarat Two-card game, largely based on luck, with the aim of getting a hand adding up to a maximum of nine points, known as a "natural." One player at a time takes on the bank. It is often given a sophisticated image, with dealers dressed in tuxedos, and played at a table away from the rest of the casino. Best places to play are Monte Carlo, MGM Grand, Aria, Encore, Bellagio, The Venetian.

Blackjack Card game, one of the many variations of Pontoon, or 21. Played at a special semicircular table, with up to seven players competing against the dealer. Best places to play are Aria, Caesars Palace, Flamingo, El Cortez, Orleans, Palms.

Craps Fast, exciting and one of the most popular games, with one player at a time rolling two dice at a special table, holding as many as 16 players, and controlled by a "boxman," who stands between the two dealers and monitors the play. To win at craps, the ultimate aim is to roll a seven. Best place to play is Casino Royale (opposite The Mirage).

Keno Similar to bingo, it originated in China. It's a very popular, easy and informal game, but with odds heavily stacked in favor of the house. Best places to play are Flamingo, Orleans, Bally's, Treasure Island.

Pai Gow Two-handed poker, based on an original Chinese domino game, with six players taking on the banker. Best places to play are Gold Coast, Orleans, The LINQ.

Roulette Possibly the most famous casino game, betting on a little ball landing in a numbered slot in a spinning wheel. It is played with special chips, with each player having a

Las Vegas is not called the entertainment capital of the world for nothing. Nevada law permits a wide variety of gaming, including traditional card and dice table

different color. If you win and want to cash in your winnings, the dealer will exchange these for winning chips, which you take to a casino cashier. Best places to play are MGM Grand, Aria, Bellagio, Mandalay Bay, El Cortez.

Slots These are sophisticated computerized machines, paying jackpots of up to $10,000 or more. Serious players guard their machines jealously—if you're playing for hours and need a food or toilet break, ask an attendant to look after your slot for you (a tip is expected). Best places to play are Aria (with the largest number and highest limits), Slots A Fun (beside Circus Circus), Palms, Gold Coast.

Texas Hold 'em Five-card game against the dealer, and currently the most popular form of poker, with betting limits from $1 to $25,000 or more. Best places to play are The Venetian, Bellagio, Rio, Golden Nugget.

Video Poker Extremely popular and fast version of the classic card game. It is played at a machine and is great if you don't want to sit down with experienced poker players. Best places to play are Palms, South Point.

Lessons
Free daytime lessons in craps, roulette and blackjack are offered at many casinos. Dealers often give advice during live games. The Excalibur and Luxor offer free poker lessons.

Do and Don't
● Choose which game to play and learn the rules first.
● Set a limit on how much you're going to spend before you start playing, and stick to it.
● Check if drinks offered by the cocktail servers are free—they often are if you're playing, but don't forget to tip.
● Keep your money in your sight and reach at all times.
● By law, players have to be 21 or older to gamble in Las Vegas casinos.

games, slot machines of virtually every type, racing and sports books, high-tech electronic gambling devices and international games of chance

Top Tips For...

These great suggestions will help you tailor your ideal visit to Las Vegas, no matter how you choose to spend your time.

Something for Free
You can't help but be drawn to the **Bellagio Fountains** (▷ 14–15).
Take a trip downtown to see the **Fremont Street Experience** (▷ 24–25), a dazzling display of images cast on an LED-light roof.
Visit one of the free, live animal attractions, such as **The Flamingo Wildlife Habitat** at the Flamingo Hotel (▷ 68).

Getting the Heart Pumping
Great for an adrenaline rush, brave the thrill rides at the **Stratosphere Tower** (▷ 56–57).
The **Big Apple Coaster** at New York New York (▷ 44–45) is an exhilarating experience.
Take to the sky in a helicopter or small plane for a bird's-eye view of the **Hoover Dam** (▷ 26–27).

Hitting the Shopping Malls
At the **Fashion Show** (▷ 68) mall you'll find the leading US department stores and more.
For a true smorgasbord of shopping deals, head for one of the outlet malls, such as **Las Vegas North Premium Outlets** (▷ 120).
Entertainment and retail therapy go hand-in-hand at **Miracle Mile Shops** (▷ 48–49).
Sample unique shopping under an artificial sky at **The Forum Shops** (▷ 16–17).
You will almost believe you are in Venice at the **Grand Canal Shoppes** (▷ 119).

Being Pampered
Travel from the airport to your hotel in a **stretch limousine** (▷ 167).
Check in at one of the most luxurious resorts, such as the **Bellagio** (▷ 14–15).
Indulge yourself in ultimate pampering at **Qua Baths & Spa** at Caesars Palace (▷ 73).

Clockwise from top: The Bellagio's spectacular dancing fountains; Caesars Palace at dusk; the lobby at Planet Hollywood; step into relaxation at Qua Baths & Spa;

Fine Dining

Dine in restaurants created by celebrity chefs—try **Jaleo** (▷ 144) at The Cosmopolitan, **Michael Mina** (▷ 146) at Bellagio and Thomas Keller's **Bouchon** (▷ 140–141) at The Venetian.

Take advantage of some of the city's finest French cuisine; **Joël Robuchon** at the MGM Grand (▷ 144) is one of the best.

High-Energy Clubs

Show your moves on the dance floor at **Marquee** (▷ 132).

For top chart hits and great views over The Strip, try **OMNIA** (▷ 133).

Experience a Vegas dayclub on summer weekends. **Encore Beach Club** (▷ 68) is still the best. Dress to impress in your best swimwear and arrive early (by noon).

For new innovations that will impress, join the sophisticated crowd at **XS** (▷ 135).

World-Class Entertainment

Lady Gaga's two-show residency at the Park Theater at MGM (▷ 158), which includes a nostalgic jazz-and-piano show, is one of the hottest tickets in town.

For a close encounter with a megastar, check out **Planet Hollywood** (▷ 48–49).

See one of **Cirque du Soleil's** breathtaking spectacles, such as *Michael Jackson ONE* (▷ 132).

Some Casino Action

Join the high rollers at **The Venetian** (▷ 58–59), watched over by Tiepolos and Titians.

The Cosmopolitan (▷ 20–21) is the foodies' casino, with some of the city's finest gourmet dining at its restaurants.

Tuxedo-backed chairs set the tone at **New York New York** (▷ 44–45), against the backdrop of the Big Apple.

a stretch limousine is one of the classic ways to get around town; views from the SkyPod at the top of Stratosphere Tower are the best in town

Timeline

1829 The spring at Las Vegas is discovered by a Mexican scout, Rafael Rivera, riding with a 60-strong trading party that had strayed from the Spanish Trail en route to Los Angeles.

1855 Mormon settlers build a fort at Las Vegas. They stay for three years, until American Indian raids drive them out.

EARLY BEGINNINGS

In prehistoric times the land on which the city stands was a marshy area that supported vigorous plant life, but the water eventually receded and the arid landscape we see today was created. However, underground water occasionally surfaced to nourish an oasis on the site where Vegas now stands, known at that time only to the area's American Indians. Archaeological finds just 10 miles (16km) northwest of Vegas have identified one of the oldest sites of human habitation in the United States. Items have been found at Tule Springs that date from around 11,000 to 14,000 years ago.

1905 On May 15, the railroad arrives, and trackside lots in what is now the Fremont Street area sell like hot cakes.

1910 Gambling is made illegal in the state of Nevada, sending the games underground.

1931 The Nevada legislature passes a bill to allow gambling, and the Red Rooster becomes the first casino to open in Las Vegas. Nevada remains the only state to allow casino gambling until 1976, when casinos are introduced to Atlantic City, New Jersey.

1940s A building boom expands Las Vegas and more casinos come to town, along with organized crime. Vegas is ruled by the Mafia behind the scenes for many decades to come.

1946 The Flamingo, one of the foremost early casinos, opens its doors. It's financed by Benjamin "Bugsy" Siegel of the Meyer Lansky gang.

"Bugsy" Siegel's Flamingo Hotel, c.1947

Demolition of the Stardust Resort and Casino on The Strip in 2007

1959 The Tropicana Hotel buys the American rights to the Parisian Folies Bergère show—it runs until 2009, with some 40,000 spectators a month.

1960s The Rat Pack (Frank Sinatra, Dean Martin, Sammy Davis Jr. *et al.*) arrive, setting the pattern for superstar entertainment.

1967 The Nevada legislature approves a bill that allows publicly traded corporations to obtain gambling licenses. Legitimate money begins to loosen the Mafia's hold.

1976 Casino gambling is legalized in Atlantic City; Las Vegas has competition.

1990s Las Vegas begins to promote family attractions. Ever bigger, more fantastic architecture starts to dominate The Strip.

1999 Wayne Newton, "Mr Las Vegas," signs a lucrative contract with the Stardust Hotel.

2005 On May 15, Las Vegas celebrates its 100th birthday.

2012 Opening of the $485-million Smith Center for the Performing Arts, which hosts Broadway, orchestral, operatic, jazz and dance shows.

2013 Caesars opens The LINQ, a giant entertainment complex on The Strip, featuring the world's tallest observation wheel (550ft/168m).

2018 Mega-resort Park MGM opens with NoMad Hotel on the top of its 32 floors.

2020 The Allegiant Stadium opens, the $1.8 billion new home of the Las Vegas Raiders NFL team.

SURPRISING ART

The entertainment capital of the world is being increasingly recognized for show-casing world-class art, whether on The Strip or the streets of Downtown, in secluded galleries or in the showiest of resorts. The longstanding Bellagio Gallery of Fine Art is still an undeniable anchor, but the once-edgy Arts District now has the city's highest concentration of galleries. Visitors can enjoy the street art and murals splashed all over Downtown or, for $100,000 a night, sleep alongside art by Damien Hirst at The Empathy Suite at Palms. Meanwhile, Clark County Government Center and the Nevada Museum of Art both delightfully celebrate the natural beauty of the desert landscape that surrounds Las Vegas.

The restaurant at the NoMad Hotel

Top 25

This section contains the must-see Top 25 sights and experiences in Las Vegas. They are listed alphabetically, and numbered so you can locate them on the inside front cover map.

★1 Bellagio

HIGHLIGHTS

● Fountain show
● Gallery of Fine Art
● Conservatory and botanical gardens
● The lobby

The Italianate image for this $1.6-billion hotel, one of the most opulent resorts in the world, was inspired by a village on the shores of Lake Como.

A touch of class An 8.5-acre (3.5ha) artificial lake at the front of the hotel sets the stage for the elegance, art and grandeur that awaits you inside. The dazzling front lobby has an 18ft (5.5m) ceiling with a central chandelier of glass flowers called Fiori di Como, designed by sculptor Dale Chihuly. All this splendor is enhanced by the wonderful botanical garden, set under a glass atrium.

Fountains of Bellagio During the computer-controlled, choreographed fountain show, millions of gallons of water are sprayed to

Clockwise from far left: View of the Bellagio from the Eiffel Tower at Paris Las Vegas; the Bellagio's pools; Dale Chihuly's spectacular lobby ceiling and chandelier of glass flowers; the plants in the conservatory change seasonally

heights of 240ft (73m) above the hotel's massive lake. The system uses individually programmed water jets and atomizing nozzles that create an atmospheric fog on the lake; some jets change the direction of the water in time to music ranging from Pavarotti to Sinatra, creating a dancing effect. At night the show is enhanced by state-of-the-art illumination and superb audio.

Over the top The casino oozes sophistication and style throughout, as even its slot machines are encased in marble and wood. Bellagio is also proud of its Gallery of Fine Art (▷ 69), and its theater was styled after the Paris Opera for Cirque du Soleil's "O" (▷ 132). The glass-enclosed Via Bellagio shopping arcade (▷ 123) has exclusive boutiques.

THE BASICS

bellagio.mgmresorts.com

➕ C9–D9

✉ 3600 Las Vegas Boulevard South

☎ 702/693-7111

◉ Fountains: Mon–Fri 3pm–midnight, Sat–Sun 12–12; every half-hour to 7 or 8pm then every 15 min (canceled in high winds); Conservatory: daily 24hr

🍴 Several cafés and restaurants $$–$$$

🚇 Bally's/Paris

🚌 Deuce, SDX

♿ Very good

💲 Fountains & conservatory: free; art gallery moderate

❓ No under-18s allowed in casino unless they are accompanied by an adult

2 Caesars Palace and The Forum Shops

- The Forum Shops mall
- Festival of Fountains
- A performance at the Colosseum
- Garden of the Gods Pool Oasis
- Qua Baths & Spa

Whether you want to shop surrounded by the historic buildings of Ancient Rome, luxuriate in one of the seven pools at the Garden of the Gods, or take sanctuary in the Roman baths of Qua Spa, Caesars Palace has it all.

Classical architecture Imagine that you have been transported to the Italian capital, amid imitative architecture that spans the period from 300BC to AD1700. The grounds are filled with reproductions of Roman statues, marble columns and colonnades, and toga-clad cocktail waitresses and costumed centurions tend to your every need in the exciting casino.

The Forum Shops Visit the phenomenal retail concourse, The Forum Shops. Browse stores

Clockwise from far left: The Fountain of the Gods; a replica of Michelangelo's David; nighttime view of the hotel; The Forum Shops

such as Burberry and Tiffany & Co., or eat at one of the many restaurants. An artificial sky overhead lightens and darkens and, every hour in the Roman Great Hall, cinematic special effects and giant animatronic statues combine to portray the struggle to rule Atlantis. All this is against a backdrop of a 50,000-gallon saltwater aquarium populated by hundreds of different species of tropical fish.

Star-studded performances The massive 4,300-seat Colosseum (▷ 130) has hosted many big-name artists over the years, including singers Céline Dion and Elton John. Other attractions reserved for hotel guests include the Garden of the Gods Pool Oasis, where you can relax, rent a cabana, enjoy a drink and play swim-up blackjack.

THE BASICS

caesarspalace.com

🔁 C8–D8

✉ 3570 Las Vegas Boulevard South

☎ 866/227-5938. The Forum Shops: 702/893-4800

🕐 Atlantis show: daily every hour 10am–10pm or 11pm

🍴 Several cafés and restaurants $–$$$

🚌 Flamingo/Caesars Palace

🚌 Deuce

🚻 Very good

🎟 Atlantis show: free

HIGHLIGHTS

● The Shops at Crystals mall (▷ 122)
● Fine art collection
● Gourmet restaurants

TIP

● Take the free tram to CityCenter which runs from the Bellagio to the Monte Carlo (daily, approx. every 15 minutes, 8am–4am; journey time 6 minutes).

This ultra-modern complex of gleaming angular towers is a self-contained city in the heart of The Strip. It's architecturally impressive, and its fine art collection is on an enormous scale.

Layout CityCenter comprises three hotels: the Aria, Vdara and the Waldorf Astoria. The site includes Crystals, the first retail center to be designed by architect Daniel Libeskind, as well as its own power plant, fire station and tram line. The complex was built paying special attention to energy conservation. For example, it uses its excess electricity to provide its hot water, and its stretch limos run on compressed natural gas—a world first. Aria has a fabulous, state-of-the-art spa featuring Japanese-style heated stone beds.

Clockwise from far left: CityCenter at night; Typewriter Eraser by Claes Oldenburg and Coosje van Bruggen; the distinctive skyscrapers of CityCenter; The Shops at Crystals mall; reflections of Las Vegas

World-class art CityCenter's towers are grouped around spacious plazas and atriums, which are decorated with artworks by several internationally acclaimed artists, such as Claes Oldenburg, Maya Lin, Richard Long, Nancy Rubins and Frank Stella. Giant aerial sculptures hang from cavernous hallways, and miniature whirlpools gyrate inside glass tubes embedded in the sidewalk. Among the most spectacular pieces are Nancy Rubins' *Big Edge*—a spiky sculpture of boats and canoes outside Vdara; Maya Lin's *Silver River*, suspended over Aria's registration desk; and a large marble sculpture by Henry Moore in the walkway, between the Aria and Crystals. The wide open public spaces offer a more relaxed experience, with modern art on display and fountains that both stimulate and soothe the senses.

THE BASICS

aria.mgmresorts.com
vdara.mgmresorts.com
waldorfastorialasvegas.com
➕ C9–D10
✉ Aria: 3730 Las Vegas Boulevard South
Vdara: 2600 West Harmon Avenue
Waldorf Astoria: 3752 Las Vegas Boulevard South
🍴 Numerous restaurants and cafés $–$$$
🚊 Bally's/Paris
🚌 Deuce
♿ Very good
🎨 Art exhibits: free

HIGHLIGHTS

● The Chandelier
● Marquee nightclub

TIPS

● Marquee nightclub also operates as a dayclub, a big trend in 24/7 Vegas.
● On some summer evenings, you can watch a movie while you swim with Dive-In Movies at the Boulevard Pool, usually at 7.30pm.

The Cosmopolitan is a gleaming, ultra-modern luxury hotel and casino, whose sophisticated amenities and bevy of edgy restaurants and nightspots reflect its fashionable, stylish image.

The building Overlooking The Strip between the Bellagio and CityCenter, The Cosmopolitan is formed of two square-sided, elegant, glass-encased towers. Inside are nearly 3,000 sumptuous boutique-style apartments, bungalows and suites. The special attractions are the nightlife and the spectacular Chandelier.

The Chandelier This shimmering cylindrical curtain contains two million glass beads, whose effect is technically enhanced with digitally programmed lighting effects. Within this fantasy

From left: The Cosmopolitan, a striking addition to the Las Vegas scene; the spectacular three-level Chandelier is unlike any bar you have ever been in

world are a bar, lounge and cocktail bar. You can choose between DJ entertainment on the bottom level, colorful cocktails in the middle, or intimately cosy sofas on the top-floor lounge.

Nightclubs, pools and more Clustered around the Chandelier are The Cosmopolitan's many amenities, both for night-owls and daytime visitors. Its hottest nightspot is the Marquee Nightclub (▷ 132), with huge four-story LED displays around its vast dance floor. For eating, choose from simple snack outlets, street food from Block 16 Urban Food Hall, and gourmet celebrity-chef restaurants. Among the top foodie venues are José Andrés' Jaleo restaurant (▷ 144), and Momofuku (▷ 146). There are also three pools, some very swanky shops and, of course, a casino.

THE BASICS

cosmopolitanlasvegas.com

🔁 D9

✉ 3708 Las Vegas Boulevard South

☎ 702/698-7000

🕐 Boulevard Pool: seasonally, hours vary; Marquee nightclub: Mon, Fri–Sat 10.30pm–4am; Marquee Dayclub: Apr–Oct daily 11.30am–sunset

🍴 Cafés and restaurants

🚋 Bally's/Paris

🚌 Deuce

♿ Very good

🎨 Art exhibits: free

21

HIGHLIGHTS

● Fremont Street
Experience (▷ 24)
● Main Street Station
(▷ 156)
● Golden Nugget (▷ 69)
● The Neon Museum
(▷ 42)
● The Mob Museum
(▷ 38)

TIP

● Some of the carts on the
Fremont Street Experience
have unusual gift and
souvenir items for sale.

With its old-world appeal, Downtown is
where Las Vegas's humble beginnings live
on through vintage casino hotels like the
Golden Gate, and two of its best museums.

Origins Focused on Fremont Street between
Main Street and Las Vegas Boulevard, the
streets of Downtown are more low-key than on
The Strip. In the 1920s, Fremont Street was
the first street in Las Vegas to be paved, and by
the 1930s it had the first licensed gaming hall.
Downtown had spent 36 years as the city's
commercial heart when the first casino resort,
El Rancho, was built on The Strip in 1941.

Revitalization Downtown lost much of its
business to The Strip by the 1990s but, since
then, the $70-million Fremont Street Experience

Clockwise from far left: Vegas Vicki sits atop the Glitter Gulch sign; the Fremont Street Experience; Sam Boyd's casino; Main Street Station Hotel has Victorian decor, antiques and blackjack tables

(▷ 24–25), along with the pedestrianized entertainment district of Fremont East, have succeeded in putting Glitter Gulch—as it is known—back on the map. Stroll in Fremont East, an atmospheric entertainment district covering six blocks, with a growing number of bars and restaurants, including Carson Kitchen (▷ 141) and the 70-year-old El Cortez casino.

More attractions With its striking Victorian decor and antiques, Main Street Station (▷ 156) has one of Downtown's best casinos. Inside the Golden Nugget casino (▷ 70), snap a photo of the Hand of Faith, an enormous (875 troy oz) gold nugget found in Australia, and The Tank, a 200,000-gallon aquarium filled with sharks and tropical fish. The Smith Center (▷ 54–55) is a state-of-the-art cultural hub.

THE BASICS
➕ G2–G3
✉ Centered around Fremont Street between Main Street and Las Vegas Boulevard
🍴 Many cafés, restaurants and snack bars $–$$$
🚌 108, Deuce
♿ Good

DID YOU KNOW?

● Fremont Street was the hub of Las Vegas for nearly four decades.
● Free live music and entertainment is on offer—check the website for details.

Head north to Downtown Las Vegas (▷ 22–23) after dark to see the only show of its kind in the world—a fantastic light-and-sound show on a massive frame that overarches a five-block area.

High-tech marvel The specifications for the initial display comprised two million light bulbs, with strobe lighting added to enhance the disco nights. A $32-million upgrade of Viva Vision—the biggest video screen in the world—made it seven times brighter.

Under cover of lightness The six-minute hourly Experience is a high-tech phenomenon with the latest computers intertwining the light, visual and audio systems. This glittering spectacular is based on a huge, solid frame that

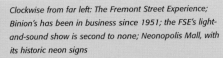

Clockwise from far left: The Fremont Street Experience; Binion's has been in business since 1951; the FSE's light-and-sound show is second to none; Neonopolis Mall, with its historic neon signs

curves 90ft (27m) above traffic-free Fremont Street, between Main and 4th streets. Several of the Downtown casinos are within this area (▷ 22–23), adding to the overall effect with their illuminated facades. There are 16 massive columns and 43,000 struts supporting the frame but, once the show starts, you will not be thinking about the engineering and instead find yourself totally focused on this zany experience, which has been wowing nighty crowds here since 1995.

By day In daylight hours, the display frame shelters a lively shopping mall, the sound system pipes in music to shop by, and there are often free concerts and street performers. SlotZilla, a zip line, 114ft (35m) above the street, offers high-adrenaline thrills (▷ 73).

THE BASICS

vegasexperience.com

✚ G3

✉ Fremont Street

☎ 702/678-5600

⏱ Shows nightly on the hour every hour from dusk to midnight (1am in summer)

🍴 Restaurants and snack bars $–$$$

🚌 Deuce, SDX, WAX

♿ Very good

✋ Free

- Guided tour into the Hoover Dam
- Cruising Lake Mead
- Crossing the Memorial Bridge

TIPS

- There is a large choice of tours available from Las Vegas (▷ 167).
- The best sightseeing cruise on Lake Mead is the one aboard the *Desert Princess*.
- Tours of the dam leave from the exhibit center at the top of the dam.

It's hard to visit Vegas without feeling some wonderment about the power it must take to light up the town. You'll find some answers at Hoover Dam, and while you're out of the city, enjoy a cruise on the lovely lake it created.

A marvel of engineering Without the Hoover Dam, Las Vegas, as we know it, would not exist. Constructed in the mid-1930s to control flooding on the Colorado River, it also provides drinking water for 18 million people and electricity for half a million homes. The Mike O'Callaghan–Pat Tillman Memorial Bridge allows visitors a bird's-eye view of the dam, a panoramic view of Lake Mead and the chance to walk into Arizona at the end of the 1,900ft (580m) crossing. Fascinating tours take visitors

Clockwise from far left: On the shores of Lake Mead; Hoover Dam, once the largest dam in the world; the dam's structural volume surpasses that of the largest pyramid in Egypt; the Desert Princess tour boat

deep inside the structure to learn more about the inner workings of one of the greatest engineering feats in history.

Lovely Lake Mead The damming of the Colorado River, beginning in 1935, created the largest artificial lake in the US at the time, with a vast 550-mile (885km) shoreline. There's a scenic drive along the western side, and the Alan Bible Visitor Center, just west of the dam, has information about waterborne activities. There are five marinas, and you can rent a boat or jet ski, go fishing, water-skiing or swimming. On dry land, there are lakeshore walks and facilities for camping and picnicking. Boulder City, near the lakeshore, was built to house the dam's construction workers and was "dry" (no alcohol or gambling).

THE BASICS

usbr.gov/lc/hoover dam; nps.gov/lake

➕ See map ▷ 109

✉ 30 miles (48km) southeast of Las Vegas

☎ Hoover Dam tours: 702/494-2517; Alan Bible Visitor Center: 702/293-8990; Lake Mead Cruises: 866/292-9191

🕐 Hoover Dam Visitor Center: daily 9–6 (5 in winter); Alan Bible Visitor Center: daily 9–4.30

✋ Hoover Dam Visitor Center Tours: expensive; Lake Mead Recreation Area: inexpensive; Lake Mead cruise: expensive

HIGHLIGHTS

● Views from the top of the High Roller
● Fly Superhero on the Fly LINQ Zipline

TIPS

● Daytime rides (before 5pm) on the High Roller are less expensive.
● Advance online tickets for the High Roller are often discounted.
● A Happy Half Hour ticket includes an open bar on the High Roller.

Rising an impressive 550ft (168m) above The Strip, Vegas's sleek High Roller currently holds the envied title of the world's tallest observation wheel.

Superlative views The High Roller changed the skyline of The Strip. It takes 30 minutes for the wheel to complete a full revolution, giving passengers ample time to soak up the 360-degree views of Las Vegas Boulevard and the desert mountains. Each of the wheel's 28 glass-enclosed cabins can hold up to 40 people. Views of The Strip's neon lights are mesmerizing at night, when the wheel is itself lit up with 2,000 LED lights.

Do it differently VIP experiences available on the High Roller wheel (which must be booked

Clockwise from far left: Fireworks light up the High Roller on 4th July; a night flight on the High Roller; high-octane views of the city from the Fly LINQ Zipline; inside one of the cabins on the High Roller

in advance) include "Yoga in the Sky," chocolate and wine tasting extravaganzas, and even wedding ceremonies inside a private cabin.

Flying high Travel 35 miles (56km) per hour, 12 stories over the LINQ Promenade on the Fly LINQ Zipline, which opened in 2018 as the latest adrenaline rush to hit Vegas. Choose from seated, Superhero or backward options on this electrifying ride that ends at the High Roller (weight and height limits apply).

Linking up High Roller and Fly LINQ are at either end of The LINQ Promenade (▷ 120), an open-air pedestrian passageway lined with boutique shops, restaurants and bars that's named for The LINQ Hotel & Casino (▷ 156) next door.

THE BASICS

caesars.com/linq

✚ D8–D9

✉ 3535 Las Vegas Boulevard South

☎ 702/322-0593; Fly LINQ: 702/777-2782

🕐 The LINQ: daily 24 hours; High Roller: daily 11.30am–2am; Fly LINQ: daily 11am–1am

🍽 Several cafés and restaurants $–$$$

🚇 Harrah's/The LINQ

🚌 Deuce

♿ Very good

💲 Expensive

HIGHLIGHTS

- *Bodies...The Exhibition*
- *Titanic* exhibition
- Replica Sphinx
- Laser light

TIP

- Save your aching feet and take the free tram to Luxor, which runs between Excalibur and Mandalay Bay every 3–7 minutes (daily, 9am–10.30pm).

Stare slack-jawed at the stunning Ancient Egyptian exterior of this vast resort. Its cavernous interior hosts two of the most imaginative and cutting-edge exhibitions in Vegas, as well as R.U.N., the newest Cirque du Soleil show.

Egyptian roots Although more modern attractions are inside, the black-glass pyramid, with its 10-floor replica Sphinx, still dominates. A spotlight shoots out of the top of the pyramid; claimed to be the strongest beam of light in the world, on a clear night it is visible from planes passing overhead.

***Titanic* docks at Luxor** *Titanic: The Artifact Exhibition* takes you on an emotional journey back in time to experience the ill-fated ship's

Clockwise from far left: For a different view of the human form, visit Bodies…The Exhibition; *an enormous Sphinx guards the entrance to the Luxor; the Digestive System exhibit; outside* Titanic *and* Bodies…The Exhibition; *take a break at the T&T Mexican-style restaurant*

maiden voyage. On display are hundreds of authentic objects recovered from *Titanic's* final resting place. A moving lifeboat enables visitors to board a reconstructed ship's bow. Walk through accurate room re-creations, share in the real-life stories of the passengers and crew, and experience the feel of an iceberg, which all sets the stage for one of history's greatest tragedies.

Come see what's inside *Bodies…The Exhibition* is a superb opportunity to see the inner workings of our bodies through actual preserved human bodies, plus more than 260 organs and partial body specimens. This daring attraction is a groundbreaking venture for Las Vegas—a fairly serious experience that will leave you with many lasting thoughts.

THE BASICS

luxor.mgmresorts.com

⊞ C11–D11

✉ 3900 Las Vegas Boulevard South

☎ 702/262 4000

🕐 *Titanic* and *Bodies* exhibitions: daily 10–10

🍴 Several cafés and restaurants

🚉 MGM Grand

🚌 Deuce

♿ Very good

💲 *Titanic* and *Bodies* exhibitions: expensive

HIGHLIGHTS

● "Music Icons"
● "The Hangover Experience"
● "Viva Vegas"
● "Marvel Superheroes"

It is fitting that Madame Tussauds' flashiest foray into the United States should be in Las Vegas, a magnet for both the biggest showbiz personalities and the most ardent celebrity-spotters.

Making an impression Madame Tussauds is the world leader when it comes to making realistic likenesses in wax of the rich, the famous and the infamous. The secret to these waxworks' life-like appearance is that they are made from an impression from the real person, rather than simply using an artist's sculpture, so every detail is absolutely spot on. Youngsters (and adults) can come face to face with classic superheroes like The Hulk and Spider-man in the Marvel Super Heroes 4D experience, which is filled with special effects and even smells.

Clockwise from far left: The star-studded cast at Madame Tussauds includes Iron Man, Louis Armstrong, Beyoncé and Marilyn Monroe

Las Vegas legends Not surprisingly, pride of place here goes to the superstars who have made their mark in Las Vegas—Wayne Newton, Elvis Presley, Céline Dion and the Rat Pack, to name just a few—but the collection regularly evolves as new stars are born. Among more than 100 other masterfully produced figures is a glittering, international cast of movie and TV stars, icons from the music world and sport's biggest achievers.

Interactive experience Some of the exhibits allow you to interact with the famous models by taking part in a scenario, such playing hoops with NBA superstar Shaquille O'Neal or stepping onto a TV studio set with Jerry Springer. Afterwards, you can hang out in *The Hangover* movie-themed bar, with views of The Strip.

THE BASICS

madametussauds.com/
las-vegas

🞢 D8

✉ The Venetian, 3377 Las Vegas Boulevard South

☎ 702/862-7800

🕐 Sun–Thu 10–8, Fri–Sat 10–9 (closes early in winter and for special events)

🍴 Several cafés and restaurants at The Venetian $–$$$

🚉 Harrah's/The LINQ

🚌 Deuce

♿ Excellent

💰 Expensive

11 MGM Grand

HIGHLIGHTS

● MGM Lion outside the main entrance
● Wet Republic
● *KÀ*, Cirque du Soleil's Egyptian-inspired extravaganza
● Joël Robuchon, 3-Michelin-star restaurant

TIP

● Hop on the monorail (▷ 167) to get to and from other major resorts.

One of the vaunted landmarks of The Strip, the MGM Grand has added an extra sparkle of Hollywood glitz since it opened in 1993.

The lion Probably the first thing you'll see when you arrive at the front entrance is the giant bronze lion statue, the instantly recognizable symbol of MGM movies since 1924. It stands 45ft (14m) tall and weighs 100,000 pounds (45,350kg).

The Grand MGM Grand is an impressive hotel casino buzzing with high-energy attractions and activities. Highlights include CSI: The Experience (▷ 67), an interactive crime-solving challenge based on the successful TV series; *KÀ* (▷ 132, panel), one of Cirque du Soleil's most thrilling shows; and Wet Republic (▷ 74),

Clockwise from far left: The entrance to the MGM Grand sports bar; the MGM Grand, with its iconic lion statue, has entertained visitors to Las Vegas for nearly 30 years; inside the lobby at the Joël Robuchon restaurant at the MGM Grand

a pool club for the city's party people. If you prefer to splash about at a more relaxed pace, you can drift along Backlot River, or pamper yourself in the Grand Spa.

Dine, dance and make merry The many dining options are headed by the Joël Robuchon restaurant (▷ 144). Hakkasan (▷ 131) offers Michelin-star-awarded Cantonese cuisine with innovative nightclub entertainment. MGM Grand Garden Arena is a major concert hall and entertainment venue, seating 16,800. It has hosted global stars, including the Rolling Stones, Bruce Springsteen, Madonna and, more recently, Lady Gaga, Coldplay and Jennifer Lopez. Sports contests also feature, including world championship boxing and basketball.

THE BASICS

mgmgrand.mgmresorts.com

🔡 D10

✉ 3799 Las Vegas Boulevard South

☎ 877/880-0880

⏱ CSI: The Experience: daily 9–9

🍴 Several cafés and restaurants $–$$$

🚇 MGM Grand

🚌 Deuce

♿ Very good

💲 CSI Experience: expensive

HIGHLIGHTS

● Volcanic eruption
● Secret Garden and white tigers
● Dolphin Habitat

Watching The Mirage's simulated volcano erupt or coming face-to-face with exotic wildlife will stop almost anyone in their tracks. Afterward, relax at the aquarium, spa or a show, all under the same roof.

TIPS

● Note that the volcano eruption will be canceled during bad weather or high winds.
● Take the free tram between Treasure Island (TI) and The Mirage (every 15 minutes, 7am–2am).

Tropical delights This Polynesian-style resort is fronted by cascading waterfalls, tropical foliage and an imitation volcano. As you enter the lobby, you can't miss the huge coral-reef aquarium stocked with tropical fish. Venture farther in and you will discover a lush rainforest under a large atrium.

Eruptions to order You can wait years for a real volcano to create its spectacle, but here, in front of The Mirage, you can set your watch by it. The spectacular 4.5-minute show starts with

Clockwise from far left: The swimming pool at the hotel; The Spa at The Mirage; the Rhumbar; The Mirage Volcano erupts on cue every evening

a rumbling sound, then a fog swirls around and a column of smoke and fire shoots more than 12ft (3.5m) into the sky. The show includes the latest special effects, with real flames on the water of the lagoon and state-of-the-art lighting techniques and sound systems, with music by Mickey Hart and Zakir Hussain. Make sure you arrive early to get a front-row position.

Other attractions The Mirage is also home to Siegfried & Roy's Secret Garden and Dolphin Habitat (▷ 73). For more wildlife viewing, seek out the 20,000-gallon saltwater aquarium, filled with 85 species of colorful tropical fish, by the hotel registration desk. The Cirque du Soleil's show *The Beatles: LOVE* (▷ 129) is presented at The Mirage and celebrates the musical legacy of the Fab Four.

THE BASICS

mirage.mgmresorts.com

✚ C8–D8

✉ 3400 Las Vegas Boulevard South

☎ 702/791-7111

🕐 Volcanic eruption: daily from 7pm (last showtime varies)

🍴 Several cafés and restaurants $–$$$

🚊 Harrah's/The LINQ

🚌 Deuce

♿ Excellent

📱 Volcanic eruption: free

HIGHLIGHTS

● The Barber's Chair—where "Murder Inc." mobster Albert Anastasia was shot dead in New York in 1957
● The wall from the 1929 St. Valentine's Day Massacre
● Speakeasy and distillery

TIP

● A special ticket is needed for The Underground tours and tastings (aged 21 or over only).

This historical museum aims to demystify the gangsters who fought for control of Las Vegas in its early days, and the lawmen who pursued them. It occupies three floors of a former federal courthouse and post office in Downtown.

Historic site Here, in 1950, the US Senate Special Committee held one of a series of nationwide hearings investigating the activities of organized crime. They found that the Capone Syndicate and New York Syndicate had turned organized crime into big business. The conclusions sent shock waves around the US, leading to the downfall of these infamous syndicates. The Mob Museum focuses on these historic events and re-creates real scenes involving the major players on both sides of the law.

Clockwise from left: The former federal building and US post office, built back in 1933, was restored to house the museum; an interactive exhibit showing the mobsters' connections; the courtroom where one of the 14 national hearings to expose organized crime took place in 1950

The Underground The distillery and speakeasy are the museum's latest attractions. Moonshine was big business for the mob during Prohibition and the star is a working still that allows visitors to taste the museum's own illicit spirits.

Skims and mayhem Displays include weapons used by mob hit-men, set against a backdrop of an iconic artifact—the wall from Chicago's St. Valentine's Day Massacre. Other exhibits show how casinos' profits were skimmed off and sent to crime syndicates' dens. Bringing Down the Mob focuses on wiretapping—one of the most important tools used to prosecute cases. Interactive exhibits let you listen to and interpret coded conversations, examine photos and surveillance films and learn about witness protection programs.

THE BASICS

themobmuseum.org

➕ G2

✉ 300 Stewart Avenue, Downtown

☎ 702/229-2734

🕐 Daily 9–9; The Underground (speakeasy and distillery) daily 9am–midnight

🚌 Deuce

♿ Very good

💰 Expensive

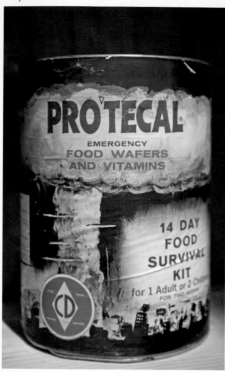

HIGHLIGHTS

- Ground Zero Theater
- A piece of the Berlin Wall
- Atomic Age cultural exhibits

This was the first museum of its kind in the US. It provides fascinating insight into scientific work done at the Nevada Test Site, starting in the wake of WWII and its subsequent global impact.

In depth Less than 2 miles (3km) east of The Strip, this national museum takes visitors on a trip through 70 years of nuclear testing. Interactive exhibits help you learn about the history of nuclear power, and you can also experience a simulated atomic explosion in the Ground Zero Theater. Other displays show you more about "backpack nukes," nuclear missiles, underground testing and different methods of radiation measurement, as well as how nuclear matters influenced pop culture and everyday life during the Cold War era.

Exhibits at the National Atomic Testing Museum documenting the history of nuclear testing at the Nevada Test Site (NTS)

Telling a story At the entrance, the ticket booth is a replica of a guard station at the historic Nevada Test Site. Located 100 miles (160km) northwest of Las Vegas out in the desert, this site was a premier proving ground for nuclear devices, and atmospheric tests were carried out there between 1951 and 1962. During that time, mushroom clouds were visible on the horizon from casinos on The Strip, where viewing parties complete with live bands and atomic-themed cocktails often were held.

Special attractions The museum's temporary exhibits take a different look at Nevada's history, sometimes from an artistic point of view or at other times with a light-hearted approach, for example, examining the alien lore surrounding mysterious Area 51.

THE BASICS

nationalatomictesting
museum.org
🚦 F9
✉ 755 East Flamingo Road
☎ 702/794-5151
🕐 Mon–Sat 10–5, Sun 12–5
🚌 202
♿ Very good
💰 Expensive

⭐ 15 The Neon Museum

HIGHLIGHTS

● Neon Boneyard tours
● La Concha Motel lobby

TIPS

● Advance booking is recommended for tours (especially night tours).
● Private events and bad weather may close the museum so check first.

Delve into Las Vegas's scandalous and storied history on a guided tour of the intriguing Neon Boneyard, a collection of more than 200 vintage signs salvaged from around the city.

Touring the collection Some of the most recognizable signs from decades past have found a new home at this outdoor museum, including Binion's lucky horseshoe, the flamboy-ant marquee from the now-departed Stardust casino and a sparkling, giant-sized high heel from the Silver Slipper casino. Daytime tours of the Boneyard are less expensive, but after-dark walks are more memorable, when a few of the restored signs are turned on and others are dramatically lit by floodlights. Tour tickets usually go on sale one month in advance.

The Neon Museum features signs from old casinos and other businesses, displayed outdoors

Get the low-down For more information and to inquire about last-minute tour availability, stop by the museum's Visitor Center, inside the refurbished La Concha Motel lobby. Designed by architect Paul Revere Williams, this shell-shaped building is an outstanding example of mid-20th-century Googie architecture.

Around Downtown If you don't have time to take a guided tour, you can still enjoy the Urban Gallery. Ten of the city's neon signs dating back to 1940 have been refurbished and displayed as installation art, on or just off Las Vegas Boulevard, between Sahara Avenue on the North Strip and Washington Avenue. More vintage neon signs are installed around the Neonopolis on the Fremont Street Experience pedestrian mall, viewable 24/7 for free.

THE BASICS

neonmuseum.org

✚ H2

✉ 770 Las Vegas Boulevard North

☎ 702/387-6366

🕐 Guided tours of Neon Boneyard offered daily (schedules vary)

🚌 113, 215

♿ Very good

💲 Moderate–expensive

HIGHLIGHTS

● Big Apple Coaster
● Statue of Liberty
● Brooklyn Bridge
● *Bliss Dance* sculpture in The Park

TIP

● You must be at least 54in (1.37m) to ride the Big Apple Coaster.

See the sights of the Big Apple in a fraction of the time you would need to explore the real thing. The Statue of Liberty, Brooklyn Bridge, the Chrysler Building—they are all here.

New York in miniature This fabulous resort hotel depicts the New York skyline through ingenious, scaled-down replicas—about one-third of the actual size—of famous Manhattan landmarks. The Statue of Liberty sits side by side with skyscrapers such as the Empire State Building and a 300ft-long (91m), 50ft-high (15m) version of the Brooklyn Bridge. The hotel's elegant art-deco lobby is set against representations of Times Square, Little Italy and Wall Street, and the casino is a nod to Central Park.

Clockwise from far left: the Center Bar is right in the middle of the gaming floor; re-creations of the Empire State Building and Statue of Liberty; a replica of the Manhattan skyline; there are plenty of places to stop for a break; hang on to your stomach!

White-knuckle ride The Big Apple Coaster twists, loops and dives at speeds of up to 67mph (108kph). The ride turns passengers upside down and inside out when the train plummets. This ride was the first to introduce the "heartline" twist and dive move, where riders experience weightlessness—the train rolls 180 degrees, suspending its passengers 86ft (26m) above the casino roof, before taking a sudden and stomach-churning dive.

The Park Just next door is a vast outdoor entertainment complex with bars, restaurants and the T-Mobile Arena for concerts and various sporting events. Rising above the crowds is *Bliss Dance*, a 40ft-tall (12m) sculpture inspired by the Burning Man festival, held in Nevada's desert.

THE BASICS

newyorknewyork.
mgmresorts.com

➕ D10

✉ 3790 Las Vegas Boulevard South

☎ 702/740-6969

🕐 Big Apple Coaster: Sun–Thu 11–11, Fri, Sat 10.30am–midnight

🍴 Several cafés and restaurants $–$$$

🚇 MGM Grand

🚌 Deuce, SDX

♿ Very good

🎢 Big Apple Coaster: moderate

HIGHLIGHTS

● Views from the Eiffel Tower Observation Deck
● Elegant shopping at Le Boulevard

Striving to capture the Parisian style of the most elegant of European cities, this hotel has succeeded in creating fine likenesses of the Eiffel Tower, Arc de Triomphe, Paris Opera House and the Louvre.

Joie de vivre This eye-catching resort reflects a characteristic French exuberance in little touches like café waiters dressed in striped shirts and berets, or maybe a "Bonjour!" from the hotel concierge.

Eiffel Tower Experience The symbol of this hotel is the 540ft (165m) Eiffel Tower (half the size of the original), which was re-created using Gustav Eiffel's blueprints. A glass elevator takes you to the observation deck on the 46th floor for spectacular views of Las Vegas

Clockwise from far left: Replicas of the Eiffel Tower and La Fontaine des Mers; neon lights; the Eiffel Tower stands out on The Strip; experience a taste of France at Le Boulevard; the elegant lobby of Paris Las Vegas

and the surrounding mountains—impressive at dusk when The Strip lights up and a prime lookout for the Bellagio fountain display opposite (▷ 14–15). A new light show (nightly every half hour; sunset–midnight), inspired by the original tower's illuminations, adds some extra sparkle to the experience.

Le Boulevard Don't miss this French-style shopping boulevard. The retail space connects Paris Las Vegas to Bally's Las Vegas (▷ 154), the resort's sister property. Amid atmospheric winding alleyways and cobbled streets, the ornate facades conceal elegant French shops, boutiques and restaurants. Weathered brickwork and brass lamps give an authentic finish, and window boxes overflowing with bright blooms complete the Parisian picture.

THE BASICS

caesars.com/
paris-las-vegas

🚹 D9

✉ 3655 Las Vegas Boulevard South

☎ 702/946-7000

🕐 Eiffel Tower Experience: Daily 9am–midnight (weather permitting)

🍴 Several cafés and restaurants $–$$$

🚆 Bally's/Paris

🚌 Deuce

♿ Very good

🎟 Eiffel Tower Experience: moderate

18 Planet Hollywood and Miracle Mile Shops

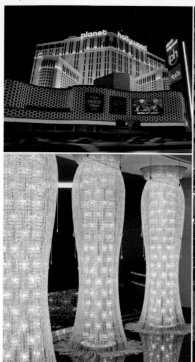

HIGHLIGHTS

● The indoor rainstorm
● The Miracle Mile Shops

Planet Hollywood has made a successful transition from Middle Eastern-themed hotel to the bright, brash style of Hollywood, with a modern feel.

Just like Times Square Massive LED signs with continually flashing images light up this part of The Strip, and when you step inside the Planet, as it's known, you will find an even more dramatic scene of highly polished black-granite floors and a color-shifting backdrop. The casino pulls in a young, stylish crowd, especially at the Pleasure Pit, where go-go girls dance above the gaming tables.

Shopping with a difference Make no mistake, Miracle Mile Shops is a shopping mall, with 170 international retailers, many eateries and a

Clockwise from far left: Outside Planet Hollywood; roulette table in the casino; you may find yourself in the middle of a rainstorm as you shop at the Miracle Mile Shops; Planet Hollywood's opulent lobby

plethora of entertainment venues, but it is not just an ordinary retail experience. It has a silver grid ceiling painted with fluffy clouds and a blue sky, which darkens during the day to complete the virtual-reality effect. While you're there, check out the latest performances at the V Theater (▷ 135), which is owned by famed producer David Saxe and hosts a huge array of shows.

Stormy weather Miracle Mile Shops is also home to the bustling Merchant's Harbor, complete with the gentle sounds of lapping waves. At intervals you will hear the rumble of distant thunder as a storm begins to brew. Clouds gather and gentle rain falls on the harbor, although you won't need an umbrella from your viewpoint on the shore.

THE BASICS

caesars.com/
planet-hollywood
miraclemileshopslv.com
➕ D9
✉ 3667 Las Vegas Boulevard South
☎ 702/785-5555
🕐 Miracle Mile Shops: Sun–Thu 10am–11pm, Fri–Sat 10am–midnight; rainstorm every hour Mon–Thu 10am–11pm, every half hour Fri–Sun 10am–11pm
🍴 Several cafés and restaurants $–$$$
🚇 Bally's/Paris
🚌 Deuce
♿ Very good

HIGHLIGHTS

● Scenic Drive
● Hiking trails
● Children's Discovery Trail
● Wildlife—burros (wild donkeys) and desert big-horn sheep (hard to spot)

TIPS

● Don't feed the wildlife; the burros may bite or kick.
● Take plenty of water if hiking—the heat can be fierce—and wear extra layers of clothes in winter.

This canyon was created 65 million years ago when the Keystone Thrust Fault pushed one rock plate up over another. The resulting formations, in gray limestone and red sandstone, are awesome.

Focal point It's incredible to think that this striking canyon, set in the beautiful 196,000-acre (79,245ha) Red Rock Canyon National Conservation Area, is a mere 30-minute drive from the razzmatazz of Vegas. The focal point is the steep red rock escarpment, more than 13 miles (21km) long and almost 3,000ft (915m) high. More canyons have been gouged out within the formation by constant snowmelt and rains, creating the present dramatic land-scape. In contrast to the dry desert, springs and streams encourage lush vegetation.

Spectacular red sandstone and gray limestone formations, along with a variety of desert vegetation, such as the Joshua tree, are distinctive features of Red Rock Canyon

Planning ahead The best place to start is at the Red Rock Canyon Visitor Center, which offers information and interpretation about all the recreational opportunities, including horseback riding, hiking and climbing. It also sells a recorded self-guided tour with a description of the geology and wildlife (all protected) in the area, and provides maps of hiking and bicycle trails and details of picnic sites. Park rangers are also on hand to give advice. Climbing should be undertaken only by experts with the correct equipment. Stick to the trails and be aware of weather conditions—flash floods do occur.

Loop the loop The 13-mile (21km) one-way Scenic Drive, leaving from the Visitor Center, lets you see some of the best rock formations and take photos at the Calico Vista viewpoints.

THE BASICS

redrockcanyonlv.org

➕ See map ▷ 108

✉ 20 miles (32km) west of L Vegas; Red Rock Visitor Center: 1000 Scenic Loop Drive

☎ 702/515-5350

🕐 Visitor Center: daily 8–4.30; Scenic Drive: Nov–Feb daily 6am–5pm, Mar & Oct 6am–7pm, Apr–Sep 6am–8pm

♿ Few

🅿 Parking: inexpensive; free for hikers. Scenic Drive: inexpensive

HIGHLIGHTS

- Sharks up to 9ft (2.75m) in length
- Underwater tunnel
- Shark, stingray and sea turtle feeds
- Touch Pool
- Golden crocodiles

TIP

- Naturalist staff are available around the pathways to help answer your questions.

Fifteen different species of shark, plus 100 other magnificent aquatic species, can be encountered close up in the imaginatively re-created marine environments of this excellent aquarium.

Massive tanks Shark Reef's 14 main exhibits contain an incredible 1.6 million gallons (6 million liters) of mineral-rich reconstituted seawater. It is home to more than 2,000 marine creatures—not only the 100 or so sharks, but also sea turtles, reptiles and fish.

The major exhibits In Shipwreck Exhibit, a sunken ship sits on the bed of a lagoon, circled by seven kinds of shark. Shoals of snapper and jack dart around, in contrast to the laidback gliding of the green sea turtles. The exciting

Clockwise from far left: Walking through the impressive underwater tunnel; getting up close and personal in the Touch Pool; a sandtiger shark; a rare shark ray; the golden crocodile is a hybrid of a saltwater and Siamese crocodile

experience of diving on a coral reef is cleverly re-created in the walk-through underwater tunnel, whose water is full of bright tropical fish to the left, right and above you. There is every probability of coming nose to nose with gray reef sharks. Elsewhere, you will see flat rays skimming through the water or resting on the "ocean" floor. The regular schedule of shark, stingray and sea turtle feeds are a definite highlight but make sure to book ahead for the best view.

Reptiles, amphibians and jungle flora Rare golden crocodiles can be found in the Crocodile Habitat (one of the few places in the western hemisphere where you can see them). In the Touch Pool you can get hands-on with stingrays and the prehistoric-looking horseshoe crabs.

THE BASICS

sharkreef.com

🔠 C11

✉ Mandalay Bay, 3950 Las Vegas Boulevard South

☎ 702/632-4555

🕐 Sun–Thu 9.30–7, Fri–Sat 10–10

🍴 Cafés and restaurants at Mandalay Bay

🚇 MGM Grand

🚌 Deuce, SDX

♿ Very good

💰 Moderate

HIGHLIGHTS

● The Grand Lobby
● Broadway-style shows
● Carillon art-deco bell tower

TIP

● There are free guided tours Mon and Sat 10am and noon (advance online booking required).

The sophisticated showpiece of Downtown's ongoing revitalization, this magnificent complex offers a world-class program of live performance of music, drama and dance.

Classic style, dynamic content The Smith Center for the Performing Arts comprises three theaters, and is the home of the Nevada Ballet Theatre and Las Vegas Philharmonic Orchestra. The complex is topped by a huge art-deco bell tower. Its largest theater is the 2,050-seat Reynolds Hall, with an orchestra pit that can hold up to 100 musicians. There is also the 250-seat Cabaret Jazz club; the 250-seat Troesh Studio Theater; and the Donald W. Reynolds Symphony Park, for outdoor concerts. Its formal hub is the Grand Lobby, a spectacular space decorated with chandeliers and artworks.

Clockwise from far left: The Carillon Tower and the eye-catching Pipe Dream Sculpture; looking down the grand central staircase; ballerinas practicing in the dance hall; state-of-the-art Reynolds Hall

High artistic aims The center's mandate is to provide a weekly program of entertainment, spanning classical, jazz, country and rock music, as well as ballet and modern dance. Global stars have included Yo-Yo Ma, Burt Bacharach and Dianne Reeves. Its Broadway hit series has featured critically acclaimed shows such as *The Phantom of the Opera* and *Motown: The Musical.*

Local roots The Smith Center is equally committed to providing an arts platform and educational facility for the local community. It is one of the partners of the Any Given Child program, which provides a long-term arts education for students in Southern Nevada. It is also the home for the DISCOVERY Children's Museum (▷ 67).

THE BASICS

thesmithcenter.com

🔳 F3

✉ 361 Symphony Park Avenue

☎ 702/749-2000 (box office)

🕐 Mon–Sat 10–6 (box office)

🍴 Several bars and snack counters

🚇 Several, including SDX and WAX, then a 5-minute walk

♿ Very good

💲 Expensive

HIGHLIGHTS

● The view from the observation deck
● A gourmet meal in the Top of the World restaurant
● The thrill rides

If zooming up the tallest free-standing observation tower in the United States isn't exciting enough for you, the highest thrill rides in the world await you at the top, along with a revolving gourmet restaurant and breathtaking views.

On top of the world Marking the northern end of The Strip, the Stratosphere stands in the shadow of its 1,149ft (350m) tower, which is the main attraction. By means of speedy double-decker elevators, you can be at the five-floor complex known as the SkyPod, which starts at 832ft (254m), in less than 40 seconds and enjoy spectacular views from the indoor observation lounge or the open-air deck. Beneath this is the revolving Top of the World gourmet restaurant (▷ 149).

Clockwise from far left: The Stratosphere Tower is an impressive piece of modern architecture; a nighttime ride on Insanity; try not to scream as X-Scream takes you over the edge; the tower is the tallest free-standing structure in the US

THE BASICS

stratospherehotel.com

E5–F5

2000 Las Vegas Boulevard South

800/998-6937

Rides: Sun–Thu 10am–1am, Fri–Sat 10am–2am

Top of the World restaurant; casino and restaurants $–$$$

SLS Las Vegas

Deuce, SDX

Very good

Tower: moderate (no charge if you have a restaurant reservation); individual rides, including admission to tower: moderate; multiride ticket: expensive

You must be at least 48in (1.22m) tall to ride the Big Shot, and 52in (1.32m) to ride X-Scream and Insanity

High-level thrills and fun Attractions at the top of the tower are not for anyone who suffers from vertigo. Big Shot, 921ft (281m) high, propels you upward at 45mph (72kph), creating a G-force of four, then plummets at zero gravity. X-Scream dangles you off the side of the building, shooting you out in a small car 27ft (8m) over the edge of the tower, some 866ft (264m) above the ground. Insanity, the ultimate in thrill rides, lets you experience centrifugal forces of three Gs while being spun 64ft (20m) beyond the edge of the tower, 900ft (274m) up. SkyJump is an 855ft (261m) stomach-lurching jump from the tower, holding the record for the highest commercial descent in the world. Alternatively, visit the AirBar, more than 800ft (244m) above The Strip, for cocktails with panoramic views.

HIGHLIGHTS

- St. Mark's Square
- Grand Canal
- Street entertainers
- Grand Canal Shoppes
- Madame Tussauds

TIPS

- Reservations for gondola rides can only be made in person on the same day.
- You will have to walk a lot to see the whole complex; wear comfortable walking shoes.

The Strip's very own replica of Venice has gone a long way to catch the flavor of this most romantic city. But at the same time it has all the glitz and pizzazz expected from Las Vegas.

Most authentic This $1.5-billion resort is one of the city's most aesthetically pleasing properties. The ornate lobby has domed and vaulted ceilings, exquisite marble floors and reproductions of frescoes framed in gold. An excellent take on Venice, it has its own 1,200ft-long (366m) Grand Canal—the real one extends 2.5 miles (4km). The waterway meanders under arched bridges, including the Rialto, and past the vibrant piazza of St. Mark's Square where living statues amaze kids with their immovable poses. Replica works of artists

Clockwise from far left: A replica of Venice's Grand Canal runs past the Grand Canal Shoppes; a café on a replica of St. Mark's Square; The Venetian at night; frescoes adorn the ceiling of the casino; gondola ride on a replica of the Grand Canal

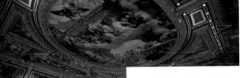

Tiepolo, Tintoretto and Titian hang in the casino. The Venetian is also home to Madame Tussauds interactive wax museum (▷ 32–33).

Gondola ride From St. Mark's, you can board a gondola and be carried down the Grand Canal to the soothing sound of water lapping against the sides; there is even a wedding gondola. Everything looks particularly spectacular at dusk, when the spirit of Venice is best captured.

Time to shop The Grand Canal Shoppes mall (▷ 119) lines an indoor cobblestoned plaza alongside the canal and is linked by walkways. There are fine restaurants and 160 interesting shops behind faux facades, while, "outside," street entertainers amuse and strolling opera singers perform Italian arias.

THE BASICS

venetian.com
✚ D8
✉ 3355 Las Vegas Boulevard South
☎ 702/414-1000. Grand Canal Shoppes/gondola ride: 702/414-4300
🕐 Gondola ride: indoor Sun–Thu 10am–11pm, Fri–Sat 10am–midnight; outdoor: daily 11–10; last ride 15 min before closing
🍴 Several cafés and restaurants $–$$$
🚉 Harrah's/The LINQ
🚌 Deuce
♿ Very good
💰 Gondola ride: expensive

24 Wedding Chapels

● Each chapel has a wedding planner for a stress-free ceremony.
● Whatever the happy couple visualize can become reality.
● Couples can get married any time of day (or night, at some chapels).

Whether your ideal wedding is being married by Elvis, tying the knot in a hot-air balloon, going for the quick drive-through ceremony or just a traditional approach, Vegas will have a chapel that can oblige.

What your heart desires Many hotels have elegant wedding chapels, or you can opt for an outdoor location amid majestic Nevada mountains and canyons. Anything goes in Las Vegas. If you're going to the chapel and you're going to get married, then the chapels lined up along Las Vegas Boulevard north of Sahara Avenue will provide a day to remember.

Gathered together in the sight of Elvis The Graceland Wedding Chapel and Viva Las Vegas Wedding Chapels offer the most renowned

Clockwise from far left: The Little White Wedding Chapel; inside the Little White Wedding Chapel; rent a stretch limo and arrive in style; just one of the wedding themes on offer at the Viva Las Vegas Wedding Chapels; Viva Las Vegas Wedding Chapels' famous pink Cadillac

style of wedding in Las Vegas, the one that's conducted by an Elvis look-alike. Graceland (▷ 70) is small, offering a more intimate experience, while Viva Las Vegas has options, such as riding into the chapel in a pink Cadillac.

Chapel of the Bells Follow in the footsteps of TV personality Kelly Ripa and soccer legend Pelé in this intimate, old-fashioned venue. Among their promotions are a candlelight ceremony and personalized wedding certificate.

Little White Wedding Chapel The setting of many celebrity weddings, the chapel is famous for its traditional ceremonies that run until after midnight—simply show up and wait your turn. The drive-through Tunnel of Love has a ceiling with painted cherubs.

THE BASICS

Viva Las Vegas Wedding Chapels
vivalasvegasweddings.com
➕ F4
✉ 1205 Las Vegas Boulevard South
☎ 702/384-0771

Chapel of the Bells
chapelofthebells
lasvegas.com
➕ F5
✉ 2233 Las Vegas Boulevard South
☎ 702/735-6803

Little White Wedding Chapel
alittlewhitechapel.com
➕ F4
✉ 1301 Las Vegas Boulevard South
☎ 800/545-8111

HIGHLIGHTS

- Waterfall and lagoon
- Lake of Dreams show
- Encore Beach Club
- Le Rêve show

This $2.7-billion resort opened in 2005, a stunning creation by Las Vegas entrepreneur and developer Steve Wynn. If you can't afford to stay here, there's nothing to stop you gazing at its magnificence.

Dazzling splendor This incredible showpiece covers 215 acres (87ha) and is one of the tallest buildings in Vegas, towering 50 stories over The Strip. The grounds are an evergreen oasis with trickling streams, the scent of fresh flowers and a newly redesigned Tom Fazio 18-hole golf course.

Spectacles for free A lagoon backed by an enormous artificial mountain, complete with a 40ft-high (12m) waterfall, takes center stage. A visual spectacular, the Lake of Dreams, is

Clockwise from far left: The elegant Parasol Down bar; the Wynn Las Vegas and its sister property, Encore, behind; Wynn Las Vegas towers above The Strip; shopping on Wynn Esplanade; the spectacular Lake of Dreams light show

projected onto the water and a screen that rises out of the lagoon. Shows run nightly every half hour. Window-shop on Wynn Esplanade (▷ 123), with its collection of designer shops, including famous European designers such as Prada, Dior, Givenchy, Louis Vuitton and Chanel.

Sensational performance The Encore Beach Club (▷ 68) is a luxurious dayclub (and night-club) offering the chance to see hot bands from the comfort of a well-stocked cabana. And try not to miss Le Rêve—an aquatic show in an aqua theater-in-the-round that dazzles with its extraordinary acrobatic feats, amazing sound-and-light effects and superb choreography. The show is named for a Picasso painting formerly owned by Steve Wynn but sold in 2013 for a reported $155 million.

THE BASICS

wynnlasvegas.com

🔳 D7–E7

✉ 3131 Las Vegas Boulevard South

☎ 702/770-7000

🎭 Lake of Dreams: shows nightly every half hour, 6pm–12.30am; Le Rêve: Fri–Tue 7 and 9.30pm

🍴 Several restaurants and cafés $–$$$

🚉 Harrah's/The LINQ

🚌 Deuce, SDX

♿ Very good

💰 Lake of Dreams: free; Le Rêve: very expensive

More to See

This section contains other great places to visit if you have more time. Some are in the heart of the city while others are a short journey away, found under Farther Afield. This chapter also has fantastic excursions that you should set aside at least a whole day to visit.

MORE TO SEE

In the Heart of the City

THE ARTS FACTORY
dtlvarts.com/arts-factory

At this complex in Downtown's 18b Las Vegas Arts District, talented local artists are showcased across some 25 galleries and studios. This is one of the main venues for First Friday events, which are held on the first Friday of each month. Galleries stay open late (6–10pm), artists display their work and street bands perform.

⊞ F4 ✉ 107 East Charleston Boulevard ☎ 702/383-3133 ⓘ Gallery and studio opening times vary; some areas are closed to the public; Barbistro: Sun 11-8, Mon–Thu 11–10, Fri–Sat 11am–midnight ▣ Deuce, SDX ⓕ Free

CANYON RANCH SPACLUB
canyonranch.com

At this deluxe spa, the theme is bliss through aquathermal rejuvenation—take your pick of a Finnish sauna, crystal steam room, a multisensory rain room, a herbal laconium, and more. A full menu of spa treatments and a state-of-the-art fitness center with group classes are available, too.

⊞ D8 ✉ Grand Canal Shoppes, The Venetian, 3355 Las Vegas Boulevard South ☎ 702/414-3600 ⓘ Daily 6am–8pm ⏹ Café and restaurant ▣ Deuce ⓕ Very expensive

CARROLL SHELBY MUSEUM
shelby.com

Part classic car museum, part auto dealership, this stop south of The Strip, near the Town Square mall, was created by legendary race-car driver and auto designer Carroll Shelby. Take a free 90-minute guided factory tour, or browse the showroom and gift shop.

⊞ Off map at D12 ✉ 6405 Ensworth Street ☎ 702/942-7325 ⓘ Mon–Sat 9.30–6, Sun 10–4; guided tours at 10.30am Mon–Sat, 1.30pm Mon–Fri ▣ SDX ⓕ Admission and tours free

CIRCUS CIRCUS
circuscircus.mgmresorts.com

Step inside the Big Top to see aerialists, acrobats, jugglers and clowns performing for free above the casino. This family-friendly resort has a roller coaster and other thrills in the Adventuredome.

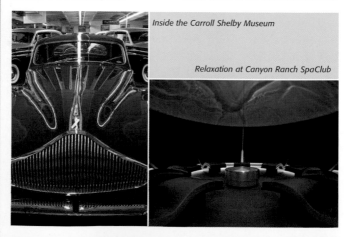

Inside the Carroll Shelby Museum

Relaxation at Canyon Ranch SpaClub

🔲 E6 ✉ 2880 Las Vegas Boulevard South
☎ 702/794-3939 ⓘ Adventuredome:
Sun–Thu 10–9, Fri–Sat 10am–midnight
🚊 SLS Las Vegas 🚌 Deuce
🎫 Adventuredome: all-day pass expensive;
individual rides inexpensive–moderate

CSI: THE EXPERIENCE
lasvegascsiexhibit.com
Based on the hit TV series, this lets
you choose from four grisly crimes
and follow clues in reconstructed
scenes, which include forensic science labs, to discover if you make
the grade as a sleuth.
🔲 D10 ✉ MGM Grand, 3799 Las Vegas
Boulevard South ☎ 702/531-3826
ⓘ Daily 9–9 🚊 MGM Grand 🚌 Deuce,
SDX 🎫 Expensive

DAYCLUBS
The city that never sleeps spawned
dayclubs–pool parties, often on
swanky hotel rooftops with big-
name DJs from Friday to Sunday.
They have all the ingredients of
nightclubs, but with added sun-
shine, swimming pools and
swimwear. Jemaa at the NoMad
(▷ 157) is an intimate affair with
inflatable flamingos and a cocktail
fountain. Marquee dayclub at The
Cosmopolitan has three-story
"townhouses" instead of cabanas.
Wet Republic at the MGM Grand
(▷ 74) is one of the oldest and
Encore (▷ 68) is still the most
popular in town.
ⓘ Usually about 11am–dusk 🎫 Expensive

DISCOVERY CHILDREN'S MUSEUM
discoverykidslv.org
Constantly changing exhibits
introduce children to the wonders
of science, communication
technology and the environment.
It's lots of fun, with interactive,
hands-on activities, and should
appeal particularly to under-5s.
There are also themed displays,
and fun experiments to try out.
The museum inhabits a large
three-story building next to the
Smith Center, in Symphony Park.
🔲 F3 ✉ 360 Promenade Place
☎ 702/382-3445 ⓘ Jun–Aug Mon–Sat
10–5, Sun 12–5; Sep–May Tue–Fri 9–4, Sat
10–5, Sun 12–5 🍴 Café Dino Mite 🚌 SDX
🎫 Moderate

MORE TO SEE

Get into character at CSI: The Experience

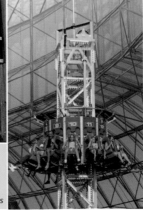

The vertical drop ride at Circus Circus

ENCORE BEACH CLUB

encorebeachclub.com

Dress to impress at this pool party, where world-famous DJs like David Guetta and Diplo spin dance music for a sexy, young crowd. Book ahead for VIP service that lets you luxuriate in a private cabana, daybed, lounger or even on an artificial lily pad.

🔳 E7 ✉ Encore Las Vegas, 3121 Las Vegas Boulevard South ☎ 702/770-7300 🕐 Fri, Sun 11–7, Sat 10–7, Mar–Sep only 🚌 Deuce, SDX 💲 Expensive–very expensive

EXCALIBUR

excalibur.mgmresorts.com

Cross the drawbridge into this fantasyland to join King Arthur and his knights. Inside you will find costumed performers and one of the most popular dinner shows: the Tournament of Kings.

🔳 D10 ✉ 3850 Las Vegas Boulevard South ☎ 702/597-7600 🕐 Tournament of Kings: Mon, Fri 6pm, Wed–Thu, Sat–Sun 6 and 8.30pm 🚌 MGM Grand 🚌 Deuce, SDX 💲 Admission free; dinner show very expensive

FASHION SHOW

thefashionshow.com

This mall is one of the country's largest and the city's premier retail destination. It is anchored by eight popular department stores: Macy's (▷ 120), Macy's Men's, Neiman Marcus, Nordstrom, Saks Fifth Avenue, Dillard's, Forever 21 and Dick's Sporting Goods. "The Cloud" structure outside acts as shade in the day and a screen at night. Fashion shows take place hourly on weekend afternoons.

🔳 D7 ✉ 3200 Las Vegas Boulevard South ☎ 702/369-8382 🕐 Mon–Sat 10–9, Sun 11–7 🍴 Numerous restaurants and cafés 🚌 Harrah's/Imperial Palace 🚌 Deuce

THE FLAMINGO WILDLIFE HABITAT

caesars.com/flamingo-las-vegas

A lush 15-acre (6ha) paradise has been recreated at the Flamingo casino hotel to house more than 300 exotic birds, such as swans, flamingos, ducks and penguins. It's a free attraction so swing by at 8.30am and 2pm daily to watch the pelicans being fed.

Indulge in some fantasy at Excalibur

GameWorks arcade

🔢 D9 ✉ Flamingo, 3555 Las Vegas Boulevard South ☎ 702/733-3111 🕐 Daily dawn–dusk 🚌 Flamingo/Caesars Palace 🚍 Deuce 💷 Free

FOUR SEASONS SPA

fourseasons.com/lasvegas/spa
Come here for luxury pampering. Treatments include facials, body scrubs, and massages, and there are two private spa suites, with sauna, steam room, whirlpool tub and massage table. The fitness center includes cardiovascular equipment and weights while the spa has saunas and Jacuzzis.
🔢 D11 ✉ Four Seasons, 3960 Las Vegas Boulevard South ☎ 702/632-5000 🕐 Spa: Mon–Fri 9–8, Sat 8–8, Sun 8–7; Fitness center: Mon–Fri 7.30am–8.30pm, Sat 6.30am–8.30pm, Sun 6.30am–7.30pm 🚍 Deuce, SDX 💷 Very expensive

GALLERY OF FINE ART

bellagio.mgmresorts.com
The first art gallery on The Strip shows a serious side to Las Vegas culture. Inside the Bellagio casino resort, this non-commercial venue showcases two small, but high-quality art exhibitions per year from major museums across the US and beyond.
🔢 D9 ✉ Bellagio, 3600 Las Vegas Boulevard South ☎ 702/693-7871 🕐 Daily 10–9, last admission 30 mins before closing 🚍 Deuce, SDX 💷 Moderate

GAMEWORKS

gameworks.com
GameWorks is the ultimate in interactive, virtual-reality arcade games. It is geared mostly to teens, although any visitor under 18 years must be accompanied by an adult (over 21) after 9pm. Located south of The Strip, it features a 225-seat restaurant, plus 125 video games, a sports bar with screens, a smoke-free bowling alley, pool tables, and eSports Gaming Center for multi-player games.
🔢 Off map at D12 ✉ Town Square, 6587 Las Vegas Boulevard South ☎ 702/978-4263 🕐 Sun–Thu 11am–midnight, Fri–Sat 11am–1am 🚍 Deuce, SDX 💷 Admission free; individual activities inexpensive–moderate

The Golden Nugget, one of Las Vegas' oldest casinos

GOLDEN NUGGET

goldennugget.com

One of Las Vegas's original casinos, the glittering Golden Nugget was built in 1946. The star attraction is The Tank—a central water feature complete with a huge 200,000-gallon (757,082-liter) shark tank. Hotel guests can slide down a transparent tube through the middle of the tank to get a closer view of its residents.

➕ G3 ✉ 129 Fremont Street ☎ 702/385-7111 🕐 Daily 24 hours. Tank viewing area: daily 10–10 🚌 Deuce, SDX 💰 Free

GRACELAND WEDDING CHAPEL

gracelandchapel.com

Couples have been marrying here for more than 70 years, and it's one of the many Elvis "shrines," where vows are taken before a look-alike of the King himself. Unless there is a wedding ceremony going on, you can look around the quaint little white-painted chapel, unmissable with its typically Vegas neon sign.

➕ G4 ✉ 619 Las Vegas Boulevard South ☎ 702/382-0091 🕐 Daily 9am–11pm 🚌 Deuce, SDX 💰 Weddings very expensive

THE GUN STORE

thegunstorelasvegas.com

Ever wanted to fire off an M16 semi-automatic rifle, a Glock pistol or a double-barreled shotgun? At this shooting range you can.

➕ Off map at H10 ✉ 2900 East Tropicana Avenue ☎ 702/454-1110 🕐 Daily 9–6.30 🚌 201 💰 Very expensive

HOLLYWOOD CARS MUSEUM

hollywoodcarsmuseum.com

Nearly 100 original automobiles and replicas used in Hollywood TV and movies are on display at this warehouse-sized space west of The Strip. Stop by to snap a photo of one of the classic American muscle cars driven in *The Fast and The Furious* movies, a James Bond submarine car, a Batmobile or the A-Team van.

➕ C11 ✉ 5115 Dean Martin Drive ☎ 702/331-6400 🕐 Daily 10–9 🚌 201 💰 Moderate

Visitors at Graceland Wedding Chapel

LAS VEGAS NATURAL HISTORY MUSEUM

lvnhm.org

Fun for families, this terrific museum provides a welcome contrast to the high life and glitz of the casinos. There are lots of interactive displays including wildlife exhibits, a small aquarium, live reptiles, scorpions and tarantulas, animatronic dinosaurs, a replica Egyptian mummy and fluorescent minerals. There are regular events, especially on weekends.

🔲 H2 ✉ 900 Las Vegas Boulevard North ☎ 702/384-3466 🕐 Daily 9–4 🚍 113 🎫 Moderate

M&M'S WORLD

mmsworld.com

An interactive retail complex over four floors with M&M's brand merchandise items, plus a 3-D movie theater, an M&M's Racing team store, and a wall covered in plain and peanut M&M's.

🔲 D10 ✉ 3785 Las Vegas Boulevard South ☎ 702/740-2504 🕐 Daily 9am–midnight 🚉 MGM Grand 🚍 Deuce, SDX 🎫 Admission and movie free

MARJORIE BARRICK MUSEUM

unlv.edu/barrickmuseum

An excellent museum devoted to contemporary art and indigenous cultures of the US Southwest and Mesoamerica from 2000BC.

🔲 G10 ✉ 4505 South Maryland Parkway ☎ 702/895-3011 🕐 Mon–Fri 9–5 (Thu till 8, Sep–Apr), Sat 12–5 🚍 109, CX 🎫 Free–donation

MARVEL AVENGERS S.T.A.T.I.O.N.

stationattraction.com

Take a leap into the world of Marvel comic books, movies and TV shows at this immersive and interactive experience that lets kids of all ages imagine training to be an agent after successfully fighting Ultron. Peruse Iron Man's high-tech suit, Captain America's uniform, Hawkeye and Black Widow uniforms and weapons, and the recreated laboratory of Bruce Banner, aka The Hulk.

🔲 D8 ✉ Treasure Island (TI), 3300 Las Vegas Boulevard South ☎ 702/766-7484 🕐 Daily 10–10, last admission 1 hour before closing 🚍 Deuce 🎫 Expensive

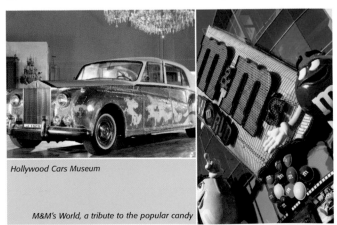

Hollywood Cars Museum

M&M's World, a tribute to the popular candy

MINUS5 ICE BAR

minus5experience.com

At one of three bars across town, take chilling to a whole new level by borrowing a parka or fake fur coat, and descending into a bar where everything —seats, chandeliers, sculptures, even your cocktail glass—is made of ice. It's an amusing novelty for such a hot climate.

➕ D11 ✉ The Shoppes at Mandalay Place, 3930 Las Vegas Boulevard South. Also at The LINQ Promenade and The Venetian ☎ 702/740-5800 ⏰ Sun–Thu 11am–2am, Fri–Sat 11am–3am 🚌 Deuce, SDX ✋ Moderate–expensive

OLD LAS VEGAS MORMON FORT

parks.nv.gov/parks/old-las-vegas-mormon-fort

The first modern people to settle the area were Mormons, who built a fort here in 1855, at a state historic park now considered "the place where Las Vegas began." The fort has been reconstructed, with one original wall surviving.

➕ H2 ✉ 500 East Washington Avenue ☎ 702/486-3511 ⏰ Tue–Sat 8–4.30 🚌 113 ✋ Inexpensive

PINBALL HALL OF FAME

pinballmuseum.org

Take a short detour east of The Strip to this nonprofit museum in a strip mall. It fills 10,000sq ft (929 sq m) and you can actually play the retro pinball machines and classic carnival and video arcade games from the 1950s through the 1990s, all lovingly restored and maintained.

➕ H10 ✉ 1610 East Tropicana Avenue ☎ 702/597-2627 ⏰ Sun–Thu 11–11, Fri–Sat 11am–midnight 🚌 201 ✋ Inexpensive

POLE POSITION RACEWAY

polepositionraceway.com

If you want a break from the casino scene, head west of the Palms casino to this superb indoor go-karting raceway, where you can floor the gas pedal and zoom around the track at thrilling speeds of up to 45mph (72kph). Drivers must be at least 56in (142cm) tall to race in adult karts.

➕ A9 ✉ 4175 South Arville Street ☎ 702/227-7223 ⏰ Sun–Thu 11–11, Fri–Sat 11am–midnight 🚌 202 ✋ Expensive

Relax in luxury at the Qua Baths & Spa

Old Las Vegas Mormon Fort

QUA BATHS & SPA

caesars.com/caesars-palace

Indulge yourself at one of The Strip's top luxury spas, complete with artificial snow falling in an ice room, saunas, whirlpool baths, plunge pools and a Men's Zone offering traditional barber services and facials. Book ahead for all the spa services and treatments: Choose from a relaxing Hawaiian lomi-lomi, Thai-style massage or a traditional Ayurvedic herbal body wrap and enjoy the expert pampering.

➕ D8 ✉ Caesars Palace, 3570 Las Vegas Boulevard South ☎ 866/782-0655 🕐 Daily 6–8 🚉 Flamingo/Caesars Palace 🚌 Deuce 💲 Very expensive

SIEGFRIED & ROY'S SECRET GARDEN AND DOLPHIN HABITAT

mirage.mgmresorts.com

Here you can see various marine mammals playing in the lagoon or get up close and personal with some of the rarest and most exotic animals in the world (including rare white lions and white tigers)

in a recreated jungle environment, all in one afternoon. Get even closer with experiences including a behind-the-scenes VIP tour, or be a "trainer for a day." Visit the Sustainability Discovery Center for details of the attraction's education and conservation programs.

➕ C8 ✉ The Mirage, 3400 Las Vegas Boulevard South ☎ 702/791-7188 🕐 Daily 10–6.30; last admission 1 hour before closing 🚉 Harrah's/The LINQ 🚌 Deuce 💲 Day pass: expensive; exclusive experiences: very expensive

SLOTZILLA

vegasexperience.com

This 12-story-high "slot-machine" tower is the launch pad from which riders can shoot up to 1,750ft (533m) down the Fremont Street Experience at speeds of up to 35mph (56kph). There are two adrenline-inducing zip lines: one at 70ft (21m) above street level, or from the upper platform at 114ft (35m).

➕ G3 ✉ 425 Fremont Street ☎ 702/678-5780 🕐 Sun–Thu 1pm–1am, Fri–Sat 1pm–2am 🚌 Deuce, SDX 💲 Expensive

Go-karting at the Pole Position Raceway

The adrenaline-inducing Slotzilla

SPA MANDALAY

mandalaybay.com

This opulent facility is a great place to relax, with views over the lagoon and gardens. In addition to all the usual spa treatments, there is a range of more exotic techniques, including a Moroccan hot stone treatment, while other amenities include whirlpools and saunas.

🔠 D11 ✉ Mandalay Bay, 3950 Las Vegas Boulevard South ☎ 702/632-7300 🕙 Daily 6am–7pm 🚇 MGM Grand 🚌 Deuce, SDX 💲 Very expensive

STRIPPER 101

stripper101.com

It's not quite what you might think—instead of being a naughty showgirl revue, this interactive pole-dancing class teaches body positivity for women of all ages, shapes and sizes. No nudity is allowed and you should bring comfy workout clothes and high heels with you.

🔠 D9 ✉ V Theater, Miracle Mile Shops, 3663 Las Vegas Boulevard South ☎ 866/932-1818 🕙 Daily (class times vary) 🚌 Deuce 💲 Expensive

"WELCOME TO FABULOUS LAS VEGAS" SIGN

Designed in 1959 by Betty Willis, this famous sign welcomes you as you enter Las Vegas at the south end of The Strip. On a lawn in the central freeway, the diamond-shaped neon sign is a popular photo stop on guided city tours, often with showgirls and Elvis look-alikes on hand for cheesy portraits.

🔠 D12 ✉ 5200 Las Vegas Boulevard South 🚌 Deuce, SDX 💲 Free

WET REPUBLIC

wetrepublic.com

Grab your swimwear and visit the MGM to enjoy two state-of-the-art saltwater pools, eight individual pools and spas, party cabanas and loungers. DJs spin hot beats and entertainers take the stage, while partygoers dance, schmooze or cool off in the water (minimum age 21).

🔠 D10 ✉ MGM Grand, 3799 Las Vegas Boulevard South ☎ 702/891-3563 🕙 Apr–Oct Thu–Mon 11–6 🚇 MGM Grand 🚌 Deuce, SDX 💲 Expensive

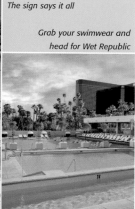

The sign says it all

Grab your swimwear and head for Wet Republic

Farther Afield

CLARK COUNTY MUSEUM

clarkcountynv.gov/parks
Explore Las Vegas's rich and varied past—its Wild West, Atomic Age, Rat Pack and beyond—in this small museum. Complete with a vintage wedding chapel and railway depot, it makes for a quick stop en route to the Hoover Dam.
⊞ See map ▷ 109 ✉ 1830 South Boulder Highway, Henderson ☎ 702/455-7955 ⊙ Daily 9–4.30 🚌 HDX
✋ Inexpensive

CLARK COUNTY WETLANDS PARK

clarkcountynv.gov/parks
Just 9 miles (15km) east of The Strip, this environmentally conscious park has a nature center where you can pick up trail maps and browse exhibits. Bird-watching is popular, and species include great blue herons, as well as many varieties of dragonflies.
⊞ See map ▷ 109 ✉ 7050 East Wetlands Park Lane ☎ 702/455-7522 ⊙ Park: daily dawn–dusk; Nature Center: daily 9–4 🚌 201, then walk 1 mile (1.5km) ✋ Free

NEVADA STATE MUSEUM

nvculture.org/nevadastatemuseumlasvegas
This museum provides a contrast to the shows and casinos. There are interactive displays, wildlife exhibits, live animals to pet, and animatronic dinosaurs. Highlights include a hands-on activity room, whales exhibition, African, marine life and robotic dinosaur galleries.
⊞ B3 ✉ 309 Valley View Boulevard South ☎ 702/486-5205 ⊙ Tue–Sun 9–5 🚌 113 ✋ Moderate; includes access to Springs Preserve

SPRINGS PRESERVE

springspreserve.org
Set in 180 acres (73ha) on the site of the original water source for Las Vegas, you can learn more about desert living via interactive displays. There are extensive gardens, trails, train rides and a butterfly habitat.
⊞ D3 ✉ 333 Valley View Boulevard South, between US95 and Alta Drive ☎ 702/822-7700 ⊙ Daily 9–5 🍴 Café 🚌 SDX from The Strip north to Downtown, then 207 westbound ✋ Moderate; includes entry to Nevada State Museum

The delightful gardens at Springs Preserve

Excursions

DEATH VALLEY

nps.gov/deva

The vast Mojave Desert sprawls for nearly 200 miles (320km) west of Las Vegas and heads across the border into North California. It makes for an adventurous day trip, with options for driving tours, hiking and bike rides.

It is the largest national park in the continental US, covering nearly 3.4 million acres (1.4 million ha). It is also the hottest and driest place in North America, with daytime temperatures regularly reaching 120°F (49°C) and rainfall averaging less than 2in (6cm) a year. It comprises a huge range of dramatic landscapes and vegetation: from its highest point at Telescope Peak, 11,049ft (3,368m) above sea level, to Badwater Basin, at 282ft (86m) below sea level—the lowest point in North America. Its geological history has produced a breathtaking array of colored rock layers, carved by erosion over millennia. Some of the best panoramas in the park are at Artist's Palette, Zabriskie Point, the Devil's Golf Course and Dante's View.

Humans settled here 10,000 years ago, and some of their descendants, the Timbisha Shoshone tribe, still maintain their ancestral homelands in protected areas. Others made their mark more recently, such as Death Valley Scotty, who lent his name to the 1920s Scotty's Castle (closed until fall 2021).

Stop by Furnace Creek Visitor Center where you can browse the natural history museum exhibits and pick up free maps and brochures. These give details of hiking trails, as well as guided activities.

Distance: 120 miles (193km) northwest of Las Vegas. From Las Vegas take Nevada State Highway 160 via Pahrump to Death Valley junction, then California State Highway 190 to northwest Furnace Creek

Journey Time: Over 2 hours

✉ Furnace Creek Visitor Center, California Highway 190 ☎ 760/786-3200 ◉ Park open 24 hours; Visitor Center daily 8–5 ♿ Moderate

Pink Adventure Tours

☎ 800/873-3662; pinkadventuretours.com

Hiking in Death Valley

Death Valley is the hottest and driest national park in the US

GRAND CANYON

nps.gov/grca

To stand on the rim of the Grand Canyon and look down to its floor below is to be confronted with raw nature at its most awe-inspiring. It's a sight that is timeless, and of which you can never tire.

The Grand Canyon stretches some 277 miles (446km) along the Colorado River, and it is this mighty river that created it, eroding the landscape over 5 million years. This erosion has revealed layer upon twisted layer of limestone, sandstone and shale, a fascinating geological cross-section of the earth's crust. At its widest point, the canyon is 18 miles (29km) from one side to the other and its deepest point is 1 mile (1.6km) beneath the rim.

The South Rim, 275 miles (443km) from Las Vegas, is the more touristy side of the canyon, because it's more accessible from elsewhere, with a rail depot and nearby airport. Grand Canyon Village here has lots of visitor facilities, including hotels, restaurants, shops and museums. In addition, this is a start point for treks into the canyon; if you have the energy, this is a wonderful way to appreciate the topography to the full.

More accessible from Vegas, only 125 miles (201km) away, is Grand Canyon West, with its famous Skywalk. The five-layered glass platform, suspended above the canyon floor, offers amazing, heart-pounding views, from 4,000ft (1,219m) up.

Distance: South Rim 275 miles (443km) from Las Vegas; Grand Canyon West 125 miles (201km) from Las Vegas

Journey Time: 3.5 hours to South Rim; 2.5 hours to Grand Canyon West

✉ South Rim Visitor Center: opposite Mather Point (about 5 miles/8km north of the south entrance station). Grand Canyon West is at the end of Diamond Bar Road, beyond Dolan Springs, off US93, 45 miles (72km) from Hoover Dam 🕐 South Rim Visitor Center: daily 9–4.30 (longer hours during peak times). Skywalk: Apr–Aug daily 7–7; Sep–Mar 8–6 💰 Skywalk: expensive ❓ It is best to take an organized tour. Many companies offer bus, helicopter and light aircraft trips from Las Vegas

The glass-bottomed SkyWalk at the West Rim of the Grand Canyon

Looking out over the canyon from the South Rim

MOUNT CHARLESTON

gomtcharleston.com

Only a short drive away and always cooler than Las Vegas—by as much as 40°F (22°C)—this lovely alpine wilderness is a joy to visit.

Located in the forested Spring Mountains, some 40 miles (65km) northwest of Las Vegas, Charleston's peak reaches 11,916ft (3,632m). It is snowcapped for more than half the year, and is sometimes even visible from The Strip. It lies within the Spring Mountains National Recreation Area, which forms part of the surrounding Humboldt-Toiyabe National Forest. Mount Charleston and its surrounding countryside are popular for their plentiful activities, including hiking (51 miles/82km of trails), horseback riding, mountain biking, rock climbing, picnicking and camping. During winter months, the US Forest Service runs various organized activities, including guided snow-shoe hikes during the weekends. There are campsites with full facilities, as well as picnic areas with hookups for RVs (caravans) and trailers.

Nearby Lee Canyon is a great spot for winter sports, including cross-country skiing and snow-shoeing. Bristlecone pines cling to the limestone cliffs, forming an awesome backdrop. The US Forest Service maintains the trails, which are suitable for all abilities. There's skiing, snowboarding and more at the family-friendly Lee Canyon ski resort (leecanyonlv.com).

At the top of Kyle Canyon, Mt. Charleston Lodge offers homey, comfortable log-cabin accommodations, good food and live entertainment in front of an open fire, with breathtaking views (mtcharlestonlodge.com).

Distance: 40 miles (65km) northwest of Las Vegas

Journey Time: 45 min

☎ 702/515-5400 🚗 Take an organized tour or go by car (check road conditions in winter). From Las Vegas, take the I-15 free-way northbound and continue to US95 north. Stay on US95 until Kyle Canyon Road, then follow signs to Mount Charleston

Mt. Charleston Lodge

Snowcapped Mount Charleston in the Spring Mountains

VALLEY OF FIRE STATE PARK

parks.nv.gov/parks/valley-of-fire

Nevada's first state park takes its name from its red sandstone rock formations, formed more than 150 million years ago by a shift in the earth's crust and eroded by water and wind. The resulting weird and wonderful shapes resemble everything from elephants to pianos. You might also be lucky enough to spot tree stumps that have survived from an ancient 250-million-year-old forest.

Note the ancient rock art (petroglyphs) by the prehistoric Basketmaker people and Early Pueblo farmers, who lived along the Muddy River between 300BC and AD1150. Petroglyphs created by these people can be seen on rocks in several sites dotted around the park, including Atlatl Rock (ask for information at the Visitor Center). Geological highlights include petrified logs, and weird sandstone formations created by erosion from wind and water, some of the best examples of which can be seen at Arch Rock and the Beehives. The varied wildlife includes roadrunners, coyotes, lizards, snakes, antelope, ground squirrels and rare desert tortoises.

You can hike along the park's well-marked trails (pick up a map, along with information at the Visitor Center), or enjoy its other activities, such as camping and picnicking. A short scenic drive from here goes up to Rainbow Vista, a lookout point with views of some of the park's most impressive colored rockscapes.

Not far from the Valley of Fire is Lake Mead (▷ 27), which, with its watersports activities and fishing opportunities, makes a good choice for a day trip.

Distance: 55 miles (88km) northeast of Las Vegas

Journey Time: 1 hour

✉ Visitor Center: 29450 Valley of Fire Road, Overton ☎ 702/397-2088 🕐 Park daily dawn–dusk; Visitor Center daily 9–4.30 💰 Moderate 🚌 Take an organized tour or go by car via the I-15 freeway northbound from Las Vegas

Rock formation caused by erosion from wind and water

Petroglyph Canyon is famous for ancient rock art

City Tours

This section contains self-guided tours that will help you explore the sights in each of the city's areas. Each tour is designed to take a day, with a map pinpointing the recommended places along the way. There is a quick reference guide at the end of each tour, listing everything you need in that region, so you know exactly what's close by.

CITY TOURS

South Strip

Expect a thrilling day of wildlife spectacles, games and white-knuckle rides. The spacious South Strip also offers some of the city's most adventurous architecture and global cuisine; from New York New York to Luxor and Mandalay Bay, you can eat your way around the world.

Morning
Start at the Showcase Mall's giant Coca-Cola bottle. Explore **M&M's World** (▷ 71) and join the line at **Tix4Tonight** (▷ 127). Then walk south of MGM Grand, guarded outside by the MGM Lion statue. Inside, cool your heels and splash into the pool party atmosphere at **Wet Republic** (▷ 67, 74), with its cosy cabanas, celebrity DJs and pool.

Lunch
Cross the walkway over The Strip to **New York New York** (left, ▷ 44–45). Ride the Big Apple around its nearly life-size skyscrapers. If you're feeling up to it after all that, have lunch at **Il Fornaio Panetteria & Restaurant** (▷ 144) Italian bakery and café, for fresh, authentic Italian pasta, pizza and *dolci*.

Afternoon
Cross the walkway over Tropicana Avenue to see **Excalibur's** (right, ▷ 68) medieval fantasy towers. Enter this multicolored castle to visit the Medieval Village. Mingle with costumed performers, dodge the fiery breath of the dragon, and have all sorts of fun exploring the traditional carnival attractions, as well as more up-to-date high-tech games or simulator rides.

Mid-afternoon

Leaving Excalibur, take a short tram ride down The Strip to **Luxor** (▷ 30–31), one of the city's most striking architectural monuments, fronted by a replica Sphinx. The *Titanic* and *Bodies* exhibitions (above) are an odd combination to find inside a life-size Egyptian pyramid, some might think, but both are hugely popular and moving in different ways. In *Titanic: The Artifact Exhibition*, you can touch a giant block of ice to help you imagine how the passengers might have felt as this huge liner sank, while *Bodies...The Exhibition* shows the inner workings of dissected and preserved human bodies.

Late afternoon

Take the tram from Luxor down to Mandalay Bay, to visit the **Shark Reef** (▷ 52–53) aquarium inside the convention center behind the hotel. This conservation-oriented feature is arranged in different habitats, with many colorful species of fish and reptiles on show, as well as 15 different species of shark. You can even immerse yourself in the experience, entering an underwater glass tunnel, from which you can watch the fish swimming over and around you.

Evening

Check out the opulent **NoMad** restaurant (right, ▷ 157) for French-American cuisine at the hotel of the same name. Soothe your aching limbs at **Spa Mandalay** (▷ 74) and round off your evening with a short taxi ride down The Strip to see the iconic **"Welcome to Fabulous Las Vegas" sign** (▷ 74). The diamond-shaped neon sign standing in the central reservation marks the start of The Strip.

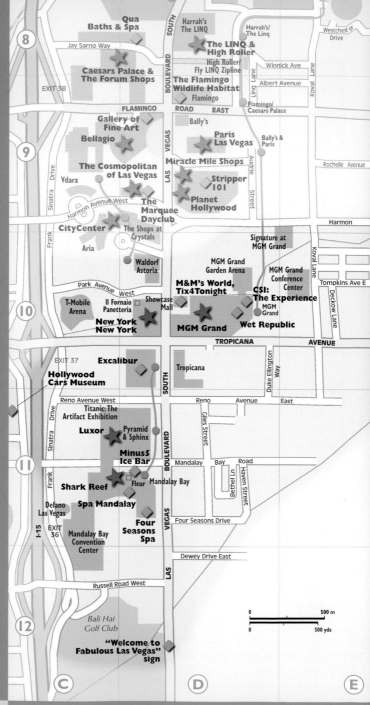

Qua
Baths & Spa

Harrah's
The LINQ

Harrah's/
The Linq

Westchest er
Drive

8

Jay Sarno Way

SOUTH

The LINQ &
High Roller

Winnick Ave

BOULEVARD

High Roller/
Fly LINQ Zipline

Albert Avenue

Lane

Burt

Koval Lane

EXIT 38

Caesars Palace &
The Forum Shops

The Flamingo
Wildlife Habitat

Flamingo

Flamingo/
Caesars Palace

FLAMINGO

ROAD

EAST

Gallery of
Fine Art

Bally's

Paris
Las Vegas

Bally's &
Paris

Bellagio

9

VEGAS

Rochelle Avenue

Miracle Mile Shops

Sinatra

Drive

The Cosmopolitan
of Las Vegas

LAS

Stripper
101

Audrie

Street

Vdara

Planet
Hollywood

Harmon Avenue West

The Marquee
Dayclub

Harmon

CityCenter

The Shops at
Crystals

Signature at
MGM Grand

Frank

Aria

Waldorf
Astoria

MGM Grand
Garden Arena

MGM Grand
Conference
Center

Koval Lane

Tompkins Ave E

Park Avenue West

M&M's World,
Tix4Tonight

CSI:
The Experience

Deckow Lane

10

T-Mobile
Arena

Il Fornaio
Panetteria

Showcase
Mall

New York
New York

MGM Grand

Wet Republic

MGM
Grand

TROPICANA

AVENUE

EXIT 37

Excalibur

Tropicana

Duke Ellington
Way

Hollywood
Cars Museum

SOUTH

Reno Avenue West

Reno

Avenue

East

Sinatra

Drive

Titanic: The
Artifact Exhibition

Giles Street

Luxor

Pyramid
& Sphinx

BOULEVARD

Mandalay

Bay

Road

11

Minus5
Ice Bar

Bethel Ln

Haven Street

Shark Reef

Fleur

Mandalay Bay

Frank

VEGAS

Spa Mandalay

Delano
Las Vegas

Four
Seasons
Spa

Four Seasons Drive

I-15

EXIT 36

Mandalay Bay
Convention
Center

LAS

Dewey Drive East

Russell Road West

Bali Hai
Golf Club

12

"Welcome to
Fabulous Las Vegas"
sign

0   500 m

0   500 yds

C   D   E

84

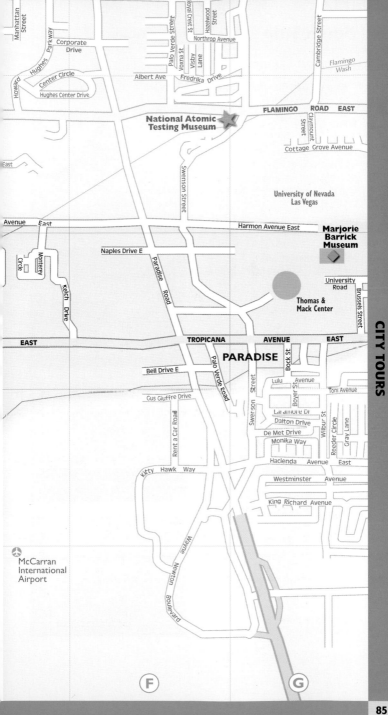

South Strip Quick Reference Guide

 SIGHTS AND EXPERIENCES

CITY TOURS

Luxor (▷ 30)
Ancient Egypt, the *Titanic* and the human body are all featured here. By night, a laser beam from Luxor's apex shoots high into the sky; it's one of the most memorable sights in Vegas.

MGM Grand (▷ 34)
Explore this homage to the movie industry; become an instant crime sleuth at CSI: The Experience; or just join the party people at Wet Republic, chilling out in the pool-side cabanas while enjoying the DJ's set.

New York New York (▷ 44)
Experience the best of the Big Apple at one-third scale, and a sky-high roller coaster. Loop the loop at high speed past the Statue of Liberty, the Empire State Building and the Brooklyn Bridge.

Shark Reef (▷ 52)
Get up close to an array of sharks, rays and rainbow shoals of colorful tropical fish from inside the glass-walled underwater tunnel at this exciting undersea world. There are experts on hand to explain the mysteries of the deep.

CITY TOURS

Center Strip

Have a romantic and visually stunning day exploring the heart of The Strip, combining traditional Vegas razzmatazz with sophisticated contemporary art and architecture.

Morning
Begin your day at **Paris Las Vegas** (▷ 46–47). Have breakfast in **Mon Ami Gabi** (right, ▷ 146), the only café with tables right on The Strip and great for people-watching over your café au lait and croque-monsieur. Ride the elevator up the Eiffel Tower for inspiring views all around the city and to the mountains beyond. Look for the thoughtfully placed lens-sized holes in the wire fence on each side of the observation platform, which allow you to take photos unobstructed.

Lunch
Take a Deuce bus up The Strip, past several casinos, including the Flamingo, to **The Venetian** (left, ▷ 58–59). Go on a gondola ride, browse the chic shops and have lunch at one of the cafés in St. Mark's Square, serenaded by performing street musicians. Live performances take place at regular intervals, with a timetable posted by the podium in the middle of the square.

Afternoon
Cross over the walkway to **The Mirage** (right, ▷ 36–37), where you can see the rare animals in **Siegfried & Roy's Secret Garden and Dolphin Habitat** (▷ 73) at the back of the resort. The dolphins are liveliest during feeding and show times, which take place throughout the day, and if you're lucky you might see one of the keepers working with the young white tigers in their enclosure.

Mid-afternoon

Turn right out of The Mirage and walk through **The Forum Shops at Caesars Palace** (right, ▷ 16–17), with its Romanesque colonnades, talking statues and stylish boutiques. On hot days, guests cool off in the Garden of the Gods: six open-air swimming pools in manicured gardens decorated with mosaics, marble tiles, statues and cabanas.

Dinner

Walk south from Caesars Palace and cross the footbridge over Flamingo Road to **Bellagio** (below, ▷ 14–15). Watch the fountain display—every 15 minutes or half an hour after dusk—to the music of perhaps Sinatra or Céline Dion. At the hotel, try the buffet, reputedly one of the best in town, or book a lakeside table at **Lago** (▷ 144).

Evening

After dinner, walk down The Strip to **The Cosmopolitan** (▷ 20–21), pausing on the way to enjoy the Bellagio's fountain show (below). Browse the uper-chic boutiques and lounges by The Cosmopolitan's main entrance. Sip a cocktail in a bar draped by the spectacular chandelier, which cascades down in the hotel's atrium. Leaving The Cosmopolitan, walk south for a few more minutes to the stunning **CityCenter** (▷ 18–19) and end the day with more upscale shopping at **The Shops at Crystals** (▷ 122) or in **Aria hotel** (▷ 153), with its casino, bars and lounges, art pieces and sculptures in the lobby.

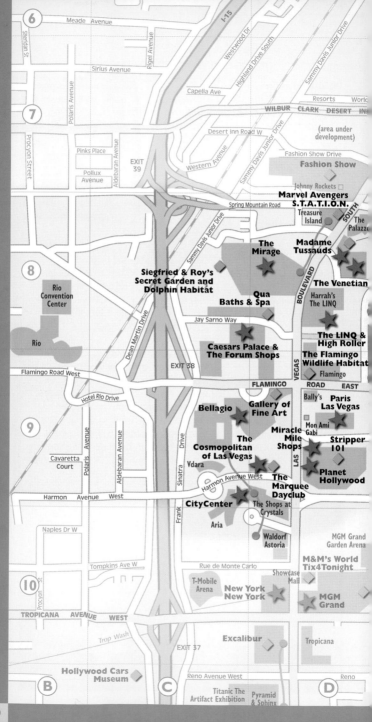

⑥ Meade Avenue I-15

Sheridan St

Rigel Avenue

Sirius Avenue

Westwood Dr

Highland Drive South

Sammy Davis Junior Drive

Capella Ave

Resorts World

⑦ WILBUR CLARK DESERT INN

Polaris Avenue

Procyon Street

Pinks Place

Pollux Avenue

Aldebaran Avenue

EXIT 39

Desert Inn Road W

Western Avenue

Sammy Davis Junior Drive

Sammy Davis Junior Drive

(area under development)

Fashion Show Drive

Fashion Show

Johnny Rockets □

Spring Mountain Road

Marvel Avengers S.T.A.T.I.O.N.

Treasure Island

The Palazzo

SOUTH

The Mirage

Madame Tussauds

⑧

Rio Convention Center

Rio

Sammy Davis Junior Drive

Siegfried & Roy's Secret Garden and Dolphin Habitat

Dean Martin Drive

Qua Baths & Spa

Jay Sarno Way

Caesars Palace & The Forum Shops

EXIT 38

Flamingo Road West

Hotel Rio Drive

FLAMINGO

BOULEVARD

Harrah's
The LINQ

The Venetian

The LINQ & High Roller

The Flamingo Wildlife Habitat

Flamingo

VEGAS

ROAD EAST

⑨

Polaris Avenue

Aldebaran Avenue

Cavaretta Court

Frank Sinatra Drive

Bellagio

The Cosmopolitan of Las Vegas

Vdara

Gallery of Fine Art

Harmon Avenue West

Harmon Avenue West

Bally's

Miracle Mile Shops

Mon Ami Gabi

Paris Las Vegas

LAS

Stripper 101

Planet Hollywood

The Marquee Dayclub

CityCenter

The Shops at Crystals

Aria

Waldorf Astoria

Naples Dr W

Tompkins Ave W

Rue de Monte Carlo

Showcase Mall

MGM Grand Garden Arena

M&M's World
Tix4Tonight

⑩

Procyon St

TROPICANA AVENUE WEST

T-Mobile Arena

New York New York

MGM Grand

Trop Wash

EXIT 37

Excalibur

Tropicana

Hollywood Cars Museum

Reno Avenue West

Reno

Ⓑ

Ⓒ

Titanic The Artifact Exhibition

Pyramid & Sphinx

Ⓓ

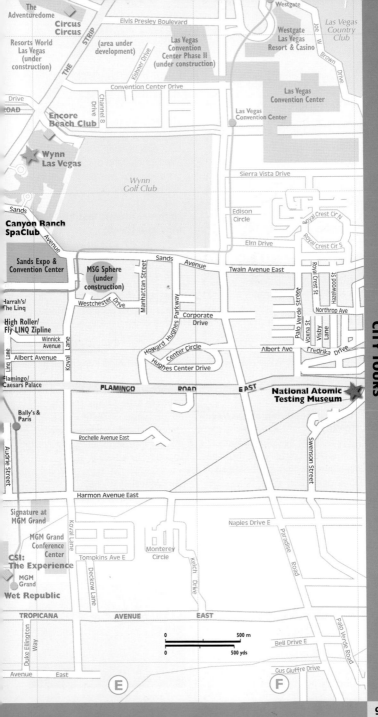

Center Strip Quick Reference Guide

TOP 25 SIGHTS AND EXPERIENCES

Bellagio (▷ 14)
This Tuscan-themed resort takes you to the Italian town on the shores of the scenic Lake Como. Its highlight is the fountain display, with soaring jets beautifully choreographed to music.

Caesars Palace (▷ 16)
Fountains and Corinthian columns celebrate the glory of Rome. This sumptuous resort is packed with fine restaurants, shopping galleries, a spa and entertainment options.

CityCenter (▷ 18)
CityCenter is a gleaming, architecturally designed complex of luxury hotels, entertainment venues and a retail center, with world-class works of fine art.

The Cosmopolitan of Las Vegas (▷ 20)
The fashionable Cosmopolitan offers stylish nightlife for the Vegas in-crowd. Don't miss the Marquee club or the bars in the three-story Chandelier.

The LINQ and High Roller (▷ 28)
Stroll along The LINQ's outdoor shopping promenade and take a sky-high ride on the world's largest observation wheel.

Madame Tussauds (▷ 32)
Wax figures of the world famous come to life in amusing scenes. Popular characters include stars who made it big in Vegas, such as Liberace and the Rat Pack.

The Mirage (▷ 36)
View exotic animals such as lions and tigers in a tropical atmosphere, and marvel at the simulated volcanic eruption in this Polynesian-themed paradise.

National Atomic Testing Museum (▷ 40)
This unique museum traces the evolution of nuclear weapons, beginning after World War II.

Paris Las Vegas (▷ 46)
The stunningly accurate half-size model of the Eiffel Tower has one of the best views over The Strip. Inside you can experience all the romance of Paris.

Planet Hollywood and Miracle Mile Shops (▷ 48)
All the glamor of Hollywood is on show in Planet Hollywood, while Miracle Mile Shops offers a relaxed shopping experience.

The Venetian (▷ 58)
Ride authentic gondolas around the canals in this elaborate indoor version of the Italian city. Marbled floors and Renaissance-style artworks adorn the lobbies and shopping arcades.

CITY TOURS

North Strip

Enjoy an action-packed day of adrenaline thrills, art and culture in this long stretch of The Strip. Combine walking with hopping on and off the Deuce double-decker bus, using its 24-hour pass.

Morning

Start your day at **The Arts Factory** (▷ 66), which has the latest in the city's alternative contemporary arts scene. On nearby blocks, you'll find unusual vintage, antiques and souvenir shops, like **Rainbow Feather Dyeing Company** and **Retro Vegas** (▷ 121). Walk east for a couple of blocks along Charleston Boulevard to The Strip and hop on the Deuce bus, passing some of Vegas' most famous **wedding chapels** (▷ 60–61), including **Viva Las Vegas** and the **Little White Wedding Chapel** (left).

Mid-morning

Get off the bus at the **Stratosphere Tower** (▷ 56–57). Ride the elevator up and go on the thrill rides, some at more than 900ft (275m) above the ground. Its latest daredevil challenge is the SkyJump: the highest controlled freefall in the world, leaping off the edge of the tower attached to a wire. Those with more sedate tastes can simply soak up the highest view in the city from the observation deck. Turn right out of the Stratosphere Tower and walk 10 minutes down The Strip to Sahara Avenue. Along the way, drop in at **Bonanza Gift Shop** (▷ 117), which claims to be the biggest souvenir shop in the world. Over the road, look for the **Chapel of the Bells** (▷ 61), one of the most popular celebrity wedding chapels.

Lunch

Jump on a Deuce bus and head south to **Circus Circus** (▷ 66–67). Ride the roller coasters (right) and watch the free circus acts inside the casino in its Adventuredome. Have lunch at one of its many snack eateries, or if you have worked up more of an appetite, gorge yourself at its buffet or on a carnivorous feast at **THE Steak House** (▷ 148).

Afternoon

Turn right out of Circus Circus and continue walking for 10 minutes down The Strip. Cross over the road to the bronze arc of **Wynn Las Vegas** (▷ 62–63), one of the most luxurious casino resorts in the city. Explore its marbled halls and exclusive shopping arcades, perhaps indulging in a cocktail or two at the magical **Parasol Down** bar (right, ▷ 133), which has pretty views over the Lake of Dreams.

Late afternoon

Crossing back over The Strip, drop into the gigantic **Fashion Show** (left, ▷ 68), for a spot of window-shopping in its glitzy boutiques and department stores. These include the famous **Macy's** (▷ 120).

Evening

Have dinner at one of the mall's many restaurants, such as the fun and lively fast-food diner **Johnny Rockets** (▷ 144). Back on The Strip, cross over the elevated walkway again and walk a few minutes north to Wynn Las Vegas to round off your evening at the Encore's **XS** (▷ 135), favored club of the city's well-heeled.

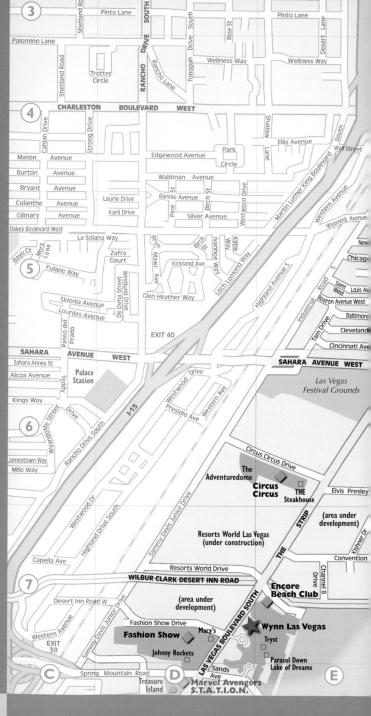

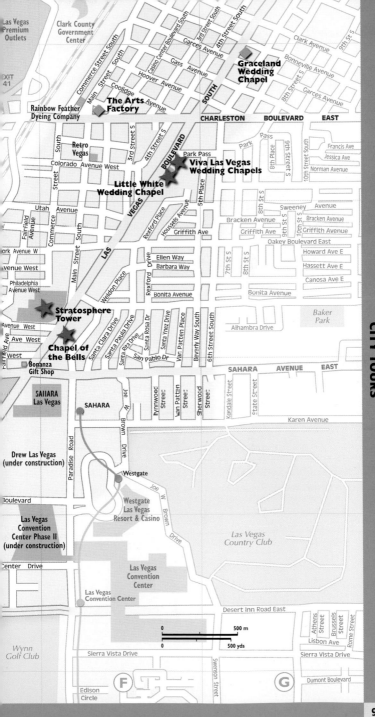

North Strip Quick Reference Guide

Stratosphere Tower (▷ 56)

For extra excitement, there are high-adrenaline rides at the top of the tallest free-standing observation tower in the US. From the platform looming more than 800ft (244m) over The Strip, you can challenge your nerves on four different rides, including SkyJump—the highest controlled freefall in the world.

Wedding Chapels (▷ 60)

Getting married in a Las Vegas wedding chapel is an event you will never forget. From driving into a chapel in a pink Cadillac with Elvis at the wheel to getting hitched in a helicopter, anything goes. You can even hire fancy dress costumes of your favorite movie characters to make it the ultimate fantasy experience.

Wynn Las Vegas (▷ 62)

This luxury resort brims with opulence. It's not just one of the tallest buildings in the city, it also has its own 18-hole golf course, a lagoon backed by an artificial mountain and even a superb collection of original masterpieces on the premises.

Downtown

Discover the city's roots at a museum dedicated to its shady mafia associations, and at an outdoor collection of some of its original neon signs. End your day here after dusk, as a blaze of neon and pounding music fills the Fremont Street Experience's arched roof.

Morning

Start at El Cortez, the only Downtown property whose exterior has remained mostly unaltered. Walk two blocks west on Fremont Street, crossing over Las Vegas Boulevard, to the Neonopolis Mall. Outside are neon signs salvaged from long-gone Las Vegas landmarks, such as Aladdin's lamp. In the outdoor atrium, the elevator shaft is encircled by vintage neon signs, too. Find even more outdoor displays of classic neon signs by walking two blocks west along the Fremont Street pedestrian mall, then north on 3rd Street. Cross over Stewart Avenue and on the next block is the old post office and federal building—a neoclassical structure built in 1933. Visit **The Mob Museum** (below left, ▷ 38–39). This major collection charts the rise and fall of organized crime in Las Vegas, in the former courthouse where a historic hearing marked the beginning of the end of the Mob gangster era.

Lunch

Continue to the end of Stewart Avenue. At the T-junction with Main Street is **Main Street Station** (above right, ▷ 156). This is one of the most floridly decorated hotels in Downtown; stained-glass windows and chandeliers add color and sparkle to its casino, and its magnificent bar has a scuplted bronze boar as its centerpiece. Have lunch at the buffet or the brewery restaurant, then pick up a map at the front desk and take a self-guided tour of the art and antiques collection.

Afternoon

Continue south along Main Street. Two blocks down on the right is the Plaza Hotel, the site of the Union Pacific railroad station, which was once the focal point of Downtown. Cross the road to the Golden Gate, one of the oldest remaining casinos and hotels in the area.

Mid-afternoon

Turn down Fremont Street under the huge canopy. Look for the neon signs, including Vegas Vic and Vegas Vickie, part of the open-air section of the **Neon Museum** (above, ▷ 42). Farther on is the **Golden Nugget** (▷ 70), Binion's and the Fremont, three of Downtown's most nostalgic casinos. You'll see people whizzing overhead on the **SlotZilla** zip line (▷ 73), Fremont Street's latest attraction.

Evening

Stay for the light-and-sound show of the **Fremont Street Experience** (right, ▷ 24–25), which fills the canopy with a blaze of color (hourly from dusk until midnight or later). Have dinner at **Binion's Café** (▷ 140), an economical option inside Binion's, or splash out at **Hugo's Cellar** (▷ 143), in the Four Queens Casino opposite.

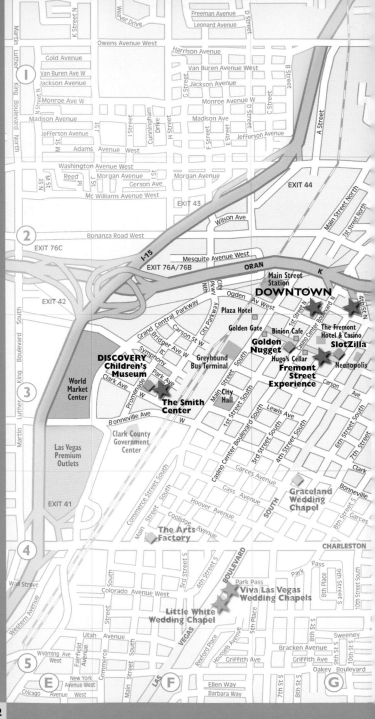

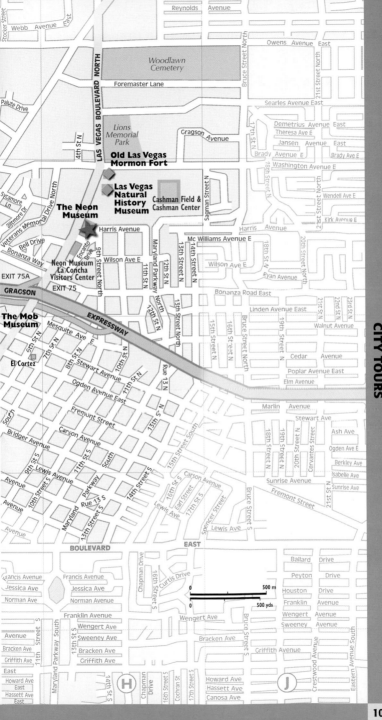

Downtown Quick Reference Guide

SIGHTS AND EXPERIENCES

Downtown (▷ 22)

If you're looking for classic Las Vegas, this is the place to find it. Iconic neon signs line the Fremont Street Experience, where you can explore some of the city's casinos.

Fremont Street Experience (▷ 24)

Be dazzled by this amazing light-and-sound show. Daily at dusk, the arched roof of Fremont Street bursts into life with two million flashing lights and stereo sound.

The Mob Museum (▷ 38)

Meet the gangsters and the law enforcement officials who finally broke the criminals' control of old Vegas. This museum is based in the original courthouse, the site of some of the showdowns.

The Neon Museum (▷ 42)

Learn all about the city's fascinating history on a guided tour of this neon sign "boneyard," filled with vintage artworks.

The Smith Center (▷ 54)

This magnificent arts complex has put Las Vegas on the cultural map, for its superb concert hall and orchestra, and by offering a year-round program of world-class music and drama.

Riding Slotzilla's adrenaline-inducing zip lines

Farther Afield

On this scenic day's drive out of Las Vegas you can witness the human wonder of the Hoover Dam, then explore Lake Mead on a winding drive around its shoreline, passing harbors, beaches and hiking trails. Arrive at Hoover Dam by 9am, as long lines for the Dam Tour form later in the morning (you can't buy tickets online, although other tours, such as the Powerplant Tour, can be purchased on the official website: usbr.gov/lc/hooverdam).

Morning
Enjoy the leisurely drive out of the city, heading south-eastward for about 30 miles (48km) to the **Hoover Dam** (left and below, ▷ 26–27). From The Strip, go west to join the I-15 south to the I-215 eastbound, picking up the I-515, which merges with US93, via Henderson after 20 miles (32km). Continue for 6 miles (10km) to Boulder City, turning left at the second set of traffic lights for another 5 miles (8km) to finally reach the turning onto Nevada State Route 172—the Hoover Dam Access Road.

Lunch
Continue on NV SR172 for 2 miles (3km) to the Dam. Park in the parking lot in the nearby Visitor Center, and take the guided tour of Hoover Dam. Have lunch afterward at the High Scaler snack bar near the Visitor Center.

Afternoon

Leaving Hoover Dam, return along the same road toward Boulder City, turning right after a few miles onto Lakeshore Road (SR 564), the scenic road running along the west side of **Lake Mead** (▷ 27), part of Lake Mead National Recreation Area. Drop in at the Alan Bible Visitor Center, just past the junction, to pick up information about visiting Lake Mead. Drive along the lakeshore, stopping along the way at designated parking spots, from where you can access lakeside paths or take a boat excursion (above). Continue around the lake; a few miles after leaving the Entrance Station take the second right-hand turn, which is signposted to Lake Las Vegas Parkway.

Mid-afternoon

Follow this short road to the Hilton Lake Las Vegas Resort & Spa (left) with its picturesque tile-roofed villas and towers, galleries and boutique shops, restaurants and marina.

Dinner

Dine at the hotel's Medici Café or at one of the informal eateries around the cobbled pathways of The Village at Lake Las Vegas.

Evening

To return to Las Vegas, continue on Lake Las Vegas Parkway, which joins I-515 northbound after about 8 miles (13km), turning right toward the city. Continue for 9 miles (15km) to the junction with Flamingo Road to continue on Lake Las Vegas Parkway back to The Strip. Alternatively, stay the night at the Hilton resort, to enjoy the lakeside tranquility and unwind in the spa and pool.

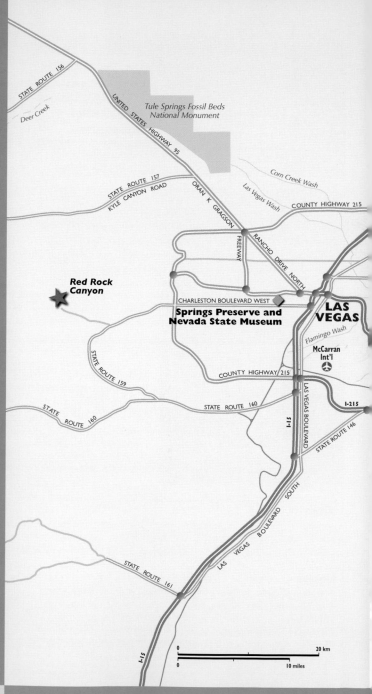

STATE ROUTE 156

Deer Creek

UNITED STATES HIGHWAY 95

Tule Springs Fossil Beds
National Monument

Corn Creek Wash

STATE ROUTE 157
KYLE CANYON ROAD

ORAN K GRAGSON

Las Vegas Wash

COUNTY HIGHWAY 215

FREEWAY

RANCHO DRIVE NORTH

**Red Rock
Canyon**

CHARLESTON BOULEVARD WEST

**Springs Preserve and
Nevada State Museum**

**LAS
VEGAS**

Flamingo Wash

**McCarran
Int'l**

STATE ROUTE 159

COUNTY HIGHWAY 215

STATE ROUTE 160

STATE
ROUTE 160

STATE ROUTE 160

I-15

LAS VEGAS BOULEVARD

STATE ROUTE 146

I-215

LAS VEGAS BOULEVARD SOUTH

STATE ROUTE 161

I-15

0   20 km

0   10 miles

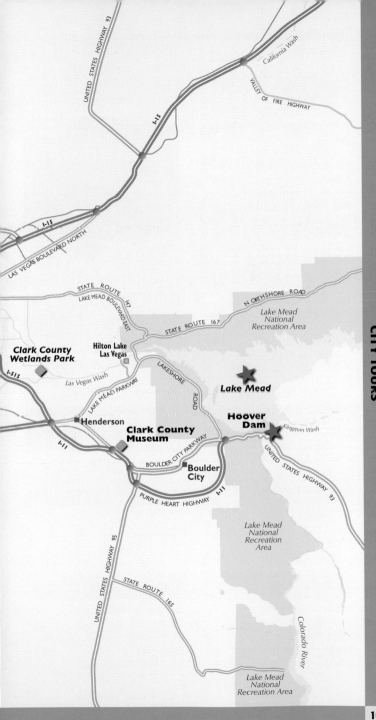

Clark County
Wetlands Park

Hilton Lake
Las Vegas

Clark County
Museum

Henderson

Boulder
City

Lake Mead

Hoover
Dam

UNITED STATES HIGHWAY 93

STATE ROUTE 167

LAKE MEAD BOULEVARD EAST

STATE ROUTE 147

N ORTHSHORE ROAD

Lake Mead
National
Recreation Area

LAKESHORE ROAD

Las Vegas Wash

LAKE MEAD PARKWAY

BOULDER CITY PARKWAY

PURPLE HEART HIGHWAY I-11

Kingman Wash

Lake Mead
National
Recreation
Area

UNITED STATES HIGHWAY 95

STATE ROUTE 165

Colorado River

Lake Mead
National
Recreation
Area

California Wash

VALLEY OF FIRE HIGHWAY

UNITED STATES HIGHWAY 93

I-15

I-15

LAS VEGAS BOULEVARD NORTH

I-515

I-11

SIGHTS AND EXPERIENCES

Hoover Dam and Lake Mead (▷ 26)

Less than an hour from the city, the Hoover Dam is one of the world's engineering wonders, and the powerhouse keeping Las Vegas going 24 hours a day. Adjacent Lake Mead, which was created by the damming of the Colorado River, offers boating, fishing and watersports.

Red Rock Canyon (▷ 50)

You'll find these spectacular rock formations only a 30-minute drive from Vegas. The striking layers of red sandstone and gray limestone, formed 65 million years ago, con-trast with the spiky desert plantlife. Today, the canyon is protected as a National Conservation Area. It forms a great setting for outdoor activities, including hiking, rock climbing and biking.

MORE TO SEE	64

Clark County Museum
Clark County Wetlands Park
Nevada State Museum
Springs Preserve

SHOP	112

Music
Sam Ash
Zia Records
Shoes and Accessories
Serge's Wigs
Silver Post USA

Shopping Malls
Las Vegas Chinatown Plaza
Town Square
Souvenirs
Las Vegas Harley-Davidson

Golf
Angel Park Golf Club
Las Vegas National Golf Club
Royal Links Golf Club

Sports and Music
Allegiant Stadium
Orleans Arena
Speed Vegas

The dazzling blue waters of Lake Mead

CITY TOURS

Dior

Shop

Whether you're looking for the best local products, a department store or a quirky boutique, you'll find them all in Las Vegas. In this section, shops are listed alphabetically.

SHOP

Introduction

Retail therapy in Vegas has soared in recent years, with an influx of designer stores and hundreds of well-known retailers and flagship department stores that have put the city firmly on the shopping map. Shopping in Vegas mainly revolves around treading the elegant walkways of the numerous malls. As for choice, it depends more on how much money you have to spend and how far you are prepared to travel than on what you are looking to buy.

A Unique Experience

Most of The Strip hotels have their own shopping opportunities, some more spectacular than others. There is simply no other city in the world where you are able to shop under an artificial sky among Roman architecture and talking statues, or journey between shops by gondola, all within a short distance of each other. Hotel malls in Vegas offer more than just great stores: all sorts of entertainment is lined up to amuse you as you shop, but this is reflected in the cost of the goods. There are other malls on The Strip not attached to any particular hotel, such as the huge Fashion Show (▷ 68).

Let's Get Serious

Serious shoppers should venture a few blocks away from The Strip, where they will discover

PAWNSHOPS

The nature of Vegas means there are lots of pawnshops. Many are Downtown and open 24 hours—ready for desperate gamblers to unload their possessions for quick cash. Items that are not reclaimed within 120 days are usually sold. You will discover all sorts of bizarre items at the pawnshops, but jewelry, musical instruments and electrical equipment are the most common. Gone are the days of acquiring items at rock-bottom prices, although you might pick up the odd bargain.

Clockwise from top: The Grand Canal Shoppes at The Venetian line a quarter-mile (400m) indoor canal; luxury shopping at Dior on Via Bellagio;

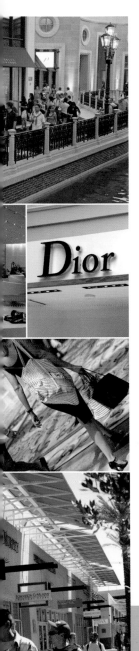

less crowded malls that are filled with major retailers and specialist stores selling practical items at more realistic prices. Clothes range from daring and on-trend to boutique exclusives, and the very latest in shoes, lingerie, jewelry and designer glasses complete a look suitable to hit the Vegas scene.

True bargainhunters should head for one of the factory outlets (▷ 120), where top designer clothes, among other things, can be bought at 25 to 75 percent off. Items for the home, electronics and footwear are particularly good value. A lot of the merchandise is end-of-line or last season's. Make sure you are getting top quality and not seconds or damaged goods. Some outlet malls have a shuttle service from hotels on The Strip.

Souvenirs and Gifts

At the other end of the scale from the classy boutiques are the endless souvenir shops along Las Vegas Boulevard, each selling the same mass-produced card decks and key rings. Every hotel also has a gift shop, with logo merchandise inspired by all the Las Vegas themes, while casino gift shops are generally more elegant and expensive.

THAT SPECIAL GIFT

Although Vegas is not known for one particular souvenir— apart from the kitsch in its gift shops—given the time and money, you can buy almost anything here. Gambling merchandise abounds in every guise and quality leather jackets bearing logos are popular. Wine makes a safe gift as Vegas has the largest public collection of fine wines in the world. You might discover that unique collectible you've always wanted—a signed Michael Jordan basketball or autographed Beatles poster. Precious jewels for sale in the city have included Ginger Rogers' engagement ring and the Mogul Mughal (one of the world's largest carved emeralds), but these might break the bank—unless you strike it lucky, of course.

---

the mosaic-tiled floor on Via Bellagio; get great discounts at Las Vegas North Premium Outlets; Gucci on Via Bellagio; La Scarpa shoe shop on Via Bellagio

Directory

SHOP

Shopping A–Z

ABERCROMBIE & FITCH

abercrombie.com

Clothing range for young aspiring men and women features the company's upscale preppy style.

➕ D7 ✉ Fashion Show, 3200 Las Vegas Boulevard South ☎ 702/650-6509 🚌 Deuce, SDX

BEBE

bebe.com

Sleek designs and curve-hugging wear inspired by the latest trends feature at this sassy boutique.

➕ D7 ✉ Fashion Show, 3200 Las Vegas Boulevard South ☎ 702/892-8083 🚌 Deuce

BONANZA GIFT SHOP

worldslargestgiftshop.com

The self-styled "largest souvenir store in the world" has a mind-boggling array of tacky mementos. It's worth a visit just to see how tasteless it can all get.

➕ E6 ✉ 2440 Las Vegas Boulevard South ☎ 702/385-7359 🚊 SLS Las Vegas 🚌 Deuce, SDX

CAROLINA HERRERA

carolinaherrera.com

Dedicated to Herrera's lifestyle collection, this store sells tailored suits, evening wear, cotton shirts and accessories.

➕ C8–D8 ✉ The Forum Shops, Caesars Palace, 3500 Las Vegas Boulevard South ☎ 702/894-5242 🚌 Deuce

CASTLE WALK

excalibur.mgmresorts.com

This mall includes gift shops selling magic tricks, medieval replica swords, shields and even armor.

➕ D10 ✉ Excalibur, 3850 Las Vegas Boulevard South ☎ 702/597-7278 🚌 Deuce

CHIHULY BELLAGIO GALLERY

chihuly.com

Chihuly opened his first gallery here, and his biggest sculpture hangs from the Bellagio's lobby ceiling (▷ 14–15). This shop has many of the respected glass sculptor's hand-blown pieces.

➕ C9–D9 ✉ Via Fiore, Bellagio, 3600 Las Vegas Boulevard South ☎ 702/693-7995 🚌 Deuce, SDX

THE COSMOPOLITAN OF LAS VEGAS

cosmopolitanlasvegas.com

Edgy, artful boutiques stock up-to-the-minute fashions, from urban street wear and custom-fitted denim to designer sneakers and swimsuits, all inside this hotel's mini shopping mall. For traffic-stopping diamond jewelry, drop into Jason of Beverly Hills.

➕ D9 ✉ 3708 Las Vegas Boulevard South ☎ 702/698-7000 🚌 Deuce

DOWNTOWN CONTAINER PARK

downtowncontainerpark.com

Come browse the crafty jewelry, all-natural beauty products and

SHOP

HOTEL SHOPPING

You will find many familiar stores in hotel malls, such as Gap, Victoria's Secret, Tommy Bahama and Levi's Original, and the classier places will have designer boutiques like Prada and Hermès, too. You won't find the big department stores here, but you'll be able to buy a good range of items, including more mundane requirements such as toiletries, cosmetics and magazines. Souvenirs may include pieces that reflect the hotel's theme, or merchandise from the permanent shows and visiting entertainers.

apparel made by young local designers. This upstart outdoor shopping mall with bar, restaurants and entertainment is a hub for an arty, young local crowd.

➕ G3 ✉ 707 East Fremont Street
☎ 702/359-9982 🚌 Deuce, SDX

FASHION SHOW

thefashionshow.com

This iconic mall contains eight department stores and more than 200 other outlets. Look out for fun fashion shows, live music and in-store demos.

➕ D7 ✉ 3200 Las Vegas Boulevard South
☎ 702/369-8382 🚌 Deuce, SDX

FIELD OF DREAMS

tristarproductions.com/fieldofdreams

This is the place for sport and celebrity memorabilia, such as a guitar signed by musician Carlos Santana or a jersey autographed by football player Dan Marino.

➕ C8–D8 ✉ The Forum Shops, Caesars Palace, 3377 Las Vegas Boulevard South
☎ 702/570-7741 🚌 Deuce

FOREVER 21

forever21.com

This huge store stocks its own-label budget casual clothing, accessories and jewelry.

➕ D7 ✉ Fashion Show, 3200 Las Vegas Boulevard South ☎ 702/735-1014
🚌 Deuce, SDX

FRUITION LAS VEGAS

casedafruition.com

This eclectic fashion store stocks everything from top designer labels to offbeat vintage apparel, all with an edgy individual flair.

➕ G9 ✉ 4139 South Maryland Parkway
☎ 702/796-4139 🚌 109, 202

GAMBLERS GENERAL STORE

gamblersgeneralstore.com

What better souvenir of your trip than something with a gambling theme? Take home a roulette wheel, blackjack table, poker chip tray or slot machine. The used card decks and gambling chips from major casinos are inexpensive.

➕ F3 ✉ 727 South Main Street
☎ 702/382-9903 🚌 108

GLAM FACTORY VINTAGE

Have fun in this down-to-earth boutique filled with retro clothes mostly from the 1940s to 70s, ranging from the funky to the outright outrageous. Look out for antiques and special events.

➕ F4 ✉ 211 East Colorado Avenue
☎ 702/443-0131 🚌 Deuce, SDX

The Forum Shops in Caesars Palace

GOLD & SILVER PAWN SHOP

gspawn.com

Join the line behind velvet ropes at this Downtown store, made famous by the reality TV series *Pawn Stars*. Filled with art, antiques, collectibles and jewelry, the showroom (where cameras are often filming) is open daily.

➕ G4 ✉ 713 Las Vegas Boulevard South ☎ 702/385-7912 🚌 Deuce, SDX

GRAND BAZAAR SHOPS

grandbazaarshops.com

This illuminated, canopied outdoor shopping mall shelters an array of accessory, beauty and one-of-a-kind specialty shops, as well as fast-food outlets. Every 15 minutes after dusk, the two-ton Swarovski Crystal Starburst dazzles during a free light, video and music show.

➕ D9 ✉ Bally's Las Vegas, 3635 Las Vegas Boulevard South ☎ 702/736-4988 🚌 Deuce

GRAND CANAL SHOPPES

grandcanalshoppes.com

This chic Italian-themed mall stretches along a replica of the Venetian Grand Canal and into The Palazzo. Here you'll find more than 100 designers, high-fashion boutiques and Barneys New York department store.

➕ D8 ✉ The Venetian & The Palazzo, 3377 Las Vegas Boulevard South ☎ 702/414-4500 🚌 Deuce

LE GRAND JEWELERS

caesars.com/ballys-las-vegas

This upscale store specializes in top-quality pearls, diamonds and gold. Sizing and fitting is offered.

➕ D9 ✉ Bally's Las Vegas, 3645 Las Vegas Boulevard South ☎ 702/736-7355 🚌 Deuce

HEXX

hexxchocolate.com

Nestled at the foot of the Eiffel Tower, this candy store is a sticky wonderland for anyone with a sweet tooth. Along with beautifully packaged bean-to-bar chocolates and candies, it has a brasserie, cocktail bar and exhibition kitchen.

➕ D9 ✉ Paris Las Vegas, 3655 Las Vegas Boulevard South ☎ 702/331-5551 🚇 Bally's/Paris 🚌 Deuce, SDX

HOUDINI'S MAGIC SHOP

houdini.com

Buy your own magic tricks from stores at New York New York, Circus Circus and The Venetian.

➕ D10 ✉ New York New York, 3790 Las Vegas Boulevard South ☎ 702/314-4674 🚇 MGM Grand 🚌 Deuce

LAS VEGAS CHINATOWN PLAZA

lvchinatownplaza.com

At this cluster of more than 20 Asian restaurants, shops and food stores, located west of The Strip, you can pick up

Asian-style ornaments, jewelry, clothes and Chinese foods. There are also plently of good-value restaurants to choose from.
➕ A8–B8 ✉ 4205 Spring Mountain Road ☎ 702/221-8448 🚌 203

LAS VEGAS HARLEY-DAVIDSON

lasvegasharleydavidson.com
One of the world's largest Harley stores has a vast array of merchandise and bikes on display for sale and to rent.
➕ D12 ✉ 5191 Las Vegas Boulevard South ☎ 702/431-8500 🚌 SDX

LAS VEGAS NORTH PREMIUM OUTLETS

premiumoutlets.com
Vegas isn't normally a place for saving money but prices are 25 to 75 percent less at this large designer and name-brand outlet, whose names include Ann Taylor, Dolce & Gabbana, DKNY, Guess, Calvin Klein, Lacoste, Adidas and Tommy Hilfiger.
➕ E3–F3 ✉ 875 South Grand Central Parkway ☎ 702/474-7500 🚌 SDX

THE LINQ PROMENADE

caesars.com/linq
Fun, colorful and casual lifestyle shops line this outdoor walkway just off The Strip. Pick up a pair of collectible sneakers at 12Am Run boutique or print your selfies at Photo & Go.
➕ D9 ✉ 3535 Las Vegas Boulevard South ☎ 800/634-6441 🚃 Harrah's/The LINQ 🚌 Deuce

M&M'S WORLD

mms.com
A tourist attraction (▷ 71) as well as a candy store and chocolate lover's dream, this place has a huge selection of well-known confectionery brands, including a vast array of liqueur-filled chocolates and, of course, M&Ms.
➕ D10 ✉ Showcase Mall, 3785 Las Vegas Boulevard South ☎ 702/740-2504 🚃 MGM Grand 🚌 Deuce, SDX

MACY'S

macys.com
This department store caters to all your fashion needs, as well as accessories, shoes and homeware.

The Shoppes at Mandalay Place offer upscale shopping and dining

MASQUERADE VILLAGE

caesars.com
Stroll down the tiled streets here
to find a range of retail outlets,
selling everything from candies
to original artwork to branded
merchandise at the Rio logo store.
✚ B8 ✉ Rio, 3700 West Flamingo Road
☎ 702/777-7777 🚌 202

PATINA DÉCOR

patinadecorlv.com
Whether it's an old gold chandelier,
a 1950s lambskin handbag or an
1980s Alexander McQueen ball
gown, this vintage interior and
clothing shop has it all, as well as
one-off and made-to-order pieces.
✚ F4 ✉ 1300 South Main Street, Suite
140 ☎ 702/776-6222 🚌 Deuce, SDX

PEARL FACTORY

pearl factory.com
See how pearls are cultured before
you pick out the ones you like, and
have them mounted in the setting
of your choice. Hawaiian heirloom
jewelry is also displayed.
✚ D8 ✉ Grand Canal Shoppes, 3377 Las
Vegas Boulevard South ☎ 702/207-0033
🚌 Deuce

PEARL MOON

mandalaybay.mgmresorts.com
It's a bit on the pricey side but it
doesn't sell pearls. Instead, the
selection of swimwear, hats,
sunglasses and sandals here is
better quality than you'll find at
many other shops on The Strip.
✚ D11 ✉ Mandalay Bay, 3950 Las Vegas
Boulevard South ☎ 702/632-6120
🚌 Deuce, SDX

RAINBOW FEATHER DYEING COMPANY

rainbowfeatherco.com
Feathers of every hue and shade
are made into boas, ornaments
and jewelry, as well as flights
for archery. The family of the late
master feather-crafter Bill Girard
creates accessories, worn by Las
Vegas showgirls and Cirque du
Soleil acrobats.
✚ F4 ✉ 1036 South Main Street
☎ 702/598-0988 🚌 108, Deuce

RETRO VEGAS

retro-vegas.com
In Downtown's 18b Arts District,
look for pink flamingos out front at
this antiques showroom specializing in mid-century modern and
vintage art, housewares, jewelry
and pocket-sized souvenirs from
Las Vegas's "Fabulous Fifties" era.
✚ F4 ✉ 1131 South Main Street
☎ 702/384-2700 🚌 108, Deuce, SDX

SAM ASH

samashmusic.com
Sam Ash is a musicians' playground, stacked high with
guitars, amps, drums and brass
and wind instruments of every
conceivable brand.
✚ H6 ✉ 2747 Maryland Parkway
☎ 702/734-0007 🚌 109

SHOP

ARTS AND CRAFTS

Las Vegas has plenty of places where
you can buy fine artworks. Classical and
contemporary art and sculpture are sold
in many shopping malls, including Fashion
Show, Forum Shops, Grand Canal
Shoppes and other outlets on and off
The Strip. The Arts Factory (▷ 66) has
many galleries and studios and holds a
special monthly late-opening evening.

On Las Vegas Boulevard between Bonanza Road and Washington Avenue is a hub of several institutions that promote art and history in the city. These include the Cashman Center, an arts and sporting center; Las Vegas Library; Las Vegas Natural History Museum (▷ 71); The Neon Museum (▷ 42); and the Old Las Vegas Mormon Fort (▷ 72), a state-owned historical park.

SERGE'S WIGS

sergeswigs.com

Choose from around 10,000 wigs and hairpieces, in all shapes and shades. Don't be surprised to find a real-life Vegas showgirl shopping beside you.

➕ A6 ✉ 4515 West Sahara Avenue ☎ 702/207-7494 🚌 SX

THE SHOPPES AT MANDALAY PLACE

mandalaybay.mgmresorts.com

A dramatic sky bridge connecting Mandalay Bay with Luxor is home to around 40 superior retailers. These include top designer names in men's and women's fashion, and renowned jewelry stores, as well as other specialties, bars and casual restaurants.

➕ D11 ✉ Mandalay Bay, 3950 Las Vegas Boulevard South ☎ 702/632-7777 🚌 Deuce, SDX

THE SHOPS AT CRYSTALS

simon.com/mall/the-shops-at-crystals

Be wowed by the angular architecture of this top-tier mall that seems to jut out into The Strip. Inside are colorfully glowing fountains, a two-story treehouse sculpture and an array of glitzy designer boutiques like Bulgari, Fendi, Dolce & Gabbana, Jimmy Choo, Tiffany & Co., Tom Ford and Stella McCartney.

➕ D9–D10 ✉ 3720 Las Vegas Boulevard South ☎ 702/590-9299 🚌 Deuce

SILVER POST USA

silverpostusa.com

A huge collection of silver jewelry is on sale, much of it handcrafted by American Indians. Items—crystals, turquoise, pottery, gemstones and cowboy boots—are of a high quality and make great gifts. There is another store downtown at Summerlin Mall.

➕ Off map ✉ 6659 Las Vegas Boulevard South, Suite 111 ☎ 702/902-2480 🚌 Deuce, SDX

TEAVANA

teavana.com

This is tea heaven and an absolute must for all aficionados of the brew. There are white, black and green varieties, plus organic, herbal and many more. The teapots, mugs, storage tins and accessories make ideal gifts for any tea lover.

➕ D7 ✉ Fashion Show, 3200 Las Vegas Boulevard South ☎ 702/369-9732 🚌 Deuce, SDX

TOMMY BAHAMA

tommybahama.com

If your prefered lifestyle is sitting on the dock of the bay, this is the store for you, with upscale beach-chic clothing for men and women, designed for that informal tropical vacation look.

➕ C8–D8 ✉ The Forum Shops, Caesars Palace, 3570 Las Vegas Boulevard South ☎ 702/933-6888 🚌 Deuce

TOWN SQUARE

mytownsquarelasvegas.com
Mediterranean and Spanish-style facades, enhanced by antique streetlights, conceal an eclectic mix of stores, restaurants and bars. A central park houses a children's playground and picnic area. There is also a cinema.
➕ Off map ✉ 6605 Las Vegas Boulevard South ☎ 702/269-5001 🚌 Deuce, SDX

VERSACE

versace.com
The late fashion designer's Italian style is obvious in the garments sold here, all made from the finest fabrics. The company's signature lion's head appears on everything.
➕ C8–D8 ✉ The Forum Shops, Caesars Palace, 3500 Las Vegas Boulevard South ☎ 702/932-5757 🚌 Deuce, SDX

VIA BELLAGIO

This opulent mall has exquisite fashion and jewelry collections from world-renowned designers Chanel, Gucci, Hermès, Louis Vuitton, Prada, Tiffany & Co. and many more.
➕ C9–D9 ✉ Bellagio, 3600 Las Vegas Boulevard South ☎ 702/693-7111 🚌 Deuce

WYNN ESPLANADE

A long list of exclusive designer names can be found at this luxury hotel mall. Get out your credit card and take your pick from the likes of Alexander McQueen, Cartier, Chanel, Louis Vuitton, Dior, Givenchy, Rolex, Salvatore Ferragamo and other luxury designer brands.
➕ D7–E7 ✉ Wynn Las Vegas, 3131 Las Vegas Boulevard South ☎ 702/770-7000 🚌 Deuce, SDX

ZIA RECORDS

ziarecords.com
The city's best independent music store is stocked with new and collectible vinyl records, CDs, movie DVDs, graphic novels, video games and books. Check the calendar for in-store celebrity appearances and live shows by bands.
➕ A6 ✉ 1216 South Rainbow Boulevard ☎ 702/233-4942 🚌 SDX

Bellagio's luxury shopping arcade, Via Bellagio

Entertainment

Once you've done with sightseeing for
the day, you'll find lots of other great
things to do with your time in this chapter,
even if all you want to do is relax with a
drink. In this section, establishments are
listed alphabetically.

Introduction

Vegas really comes alive after the sun goes down, and some of the best attractions are to be found during the twilight hours. Soak up a pulsating nightlife scene like no other—this is a great place to party.

Endless Variety

From casino lounges to clubs, pubs and cocktail bars, the possibilities for a fun night out are endless. Numerous nightspots provide the chance to dance until dawn. Ultra lounges are the latest trend, stylish spaces that attract a cutting-edge crowd, where DJs spin their vinyl but conversation takes priority. But this is Sin City, and there are several not very well-concealed strip joints scattered throughout. These can, however, be disregarded amid the sheer scale of everything else.

Only the Best

Las Vegas is infamous for its spectacularly staged extravaganzas, which incorporate unbelievable special effects and have attracted some of the world's hottest superstars. Shows vary from Broadway musicals and spectacular productions to comedy and magic. Vegas also plays host to some of the world's biggest special events, such as world championship boxing matches. The top shows can be expensive and the most popular often need to be reserved well in advance. But the best

GAMING

Where else could you continually be refueled with free drinks as you play the blackjack table or wait for the roulette wheel to stop spinning? But be careful not to lose it all in one night. If you're not a serious player, the slot machines are lots of fun, too. Strolling through the casinos people-watching is another great way to pass the time—weary gamblers desperately trying to claw back some of their losses, ecstatic cries of joy when their luck holds and the jangling of chips when the slots pay out.

Clockwise from top: The House of Blues, Mandalay Bay Resort; cocktail bar at Mandalay Bay; the Zebras from the Bellagio's "O"; you can enjoy a cocktail any time;

show of all is free: walk The Strip after dark and be treated to the amazing performance of thousands of flashing neon lights.

From Highbrow to Fringe

With the ongoing regeneration of Downtown, a wider range of arts and culture has added to the dazzling spectacle that is The Strip's traditional fare. The Smith Center (▷ 54–55) is a major architectural complex that houses the Nevada Ballet Theatre and Las Vegas Philharmonic. It offers a program of world-class live performances. The fringe music scene is also very much alive and growing, with open-mike sessions and acoustic gigs at various venues, mostly Downtown in the Fremont East Entertainment District and the 18b Arts District.

Discount Tickets

Top show tickets can cost upward of $100, but you can make big savings at discount agencies and with coupons in the free tourist magazines. Tix4Tonight (tix4tonight.com) offers up to half-price tickets for same-day shows, with kiosks on Mid-Strip at Bally's Grand Bazaar Shops, Planet Hollywood and Casino Royale; also Downtown at the Four Queens on Fremont Street; and the Fashion Show mall; and South Strip at the Showcase Mall next to the giant Coca-Cola bottle. Shows on offer are typically listed at 9.30 daily, with tickets on sale from 10–7 or later, or tel 877/849-4868.

WEIRD AND WACKY

Las Vegas is constantly coming up with increasingly adventurous and sometimes edgy shows. Several hypnosis acts invite volunteers from the audience on stage to commit hilarious acts that border on the lewd. Audience participation is ever popular: Take front row seats at your peril. Subtle it ain't, but mainstream shows on The Strip are all about doing it loud and large.

synchronized swimmers in Bellagio's "O" performance; Le Rêve, Wynn Las Vegas

Directory

Entertainment A–Z

107 SKY LOUNGE
topoftheworldlv.com
Visit this sophisticated cocktail
lounge bar before or after a meal
at the Top of the World restaurant
(▷ 149). High up on the 107th
floor, it offers a 360-degree view
of the Las Vegas skyline. Martinis
are the house specialty.
✚ E5–F5 ✉ Stratosphere, 2000 Las
Vegas Boulevard South ☎ 702/380-7711
⏰ Daily 4pm–3am 🚇 Deuce 💵 No
cover charge

ABSINTHE
spiegelworld.com
This thrilling show in-the-round
is highly acclaimed for its jaw-
dropping acrobatics, combined
with equally outrageous burlesque
comedy. In either case, it's not one
for the fainthearted.
✚ C8–D8 ✉ Roman Plaza, Caesars Palace,
3570 Las Vegas Boulevard South
☎ 702/893-4800 ⏰ Wed–Sun 8pm and
10pm 🚇 Flamingo/Caesars Palace
🚇 Deuce 💵 Very expensive

ALLEGIANT STADIUM

allegiantstadium.com
NFL Oakland Raiders relocated to Las Vegas in 2020 to this $750-million, 65,000-seat stadium, which also hosts the Las Vegas Bowl, the Pac-12 Football Championship and other major sporting events.

➕ Off map ✉ 3333 Al Davis Way
🕐 Opening hours vary according to games
🚌 MGM Grand 🚍 Deuce, SDX 💷 Varies

ANGEL PARK GOLF CLUB

angelpark.com
Experience both mountains and palms at this 36-hole course designed by legendary golfer Arnold Palmer. There are spectacular views over Red Rock Canyon and the Las Vegas Valley.

➕ Off map ✉ 100 South Rampart Boulevard, west of US95 and south of Summerlin Parkway ☎ 888/446-5358
🕐 Daily (opening hours vary) 🚍 WAX
💷 Very expensive

BALI HAI GOLF CLUB

balihaigolfclub.com
A South Pacific theme runs throughout this 18-hole championship course off the southern end of The Strip, with outcrops of volcanic rock, palm trees and white sand bunkers.

➕ C12–D12 ✉ 5160 Las Vegas Boulevard South ☎ 866/330-5211 🕐 Daily (opening hours vary) 🚍 SDX 💷 Very expensive

THE BEATLES: LOVE

cirquedusoleil.com
Cirque du Soleil's production, *LOVE* celebrates the Beatles' legacy and explores their songs in scenes inhabited by real and imaginary people, all accompanied by acrobatics and dancing.

➕ D8 ✉ The Mirage, 3400 Las Vegas Boulevard South ☎ 702/792-7777
🕐 Thu–Mon 7pm and 9.30pm
🚌 Harrah's/The LINQ 🚍 Deuce
💷 Very expensive

BLUE MAN GROUP

blueman.com
One of the most unusual shows in Vegas, this group of guys with cobalt-blue bald heads performs hilarious routines, creating artistic canvases by the strangest means.

➕ D11 ✉ Luxor, 3900 Las Vegas Boulevard South ☎ 702/262-4200
🕐 Daily 7pm and 9.30pm 🚍 Deuce
💷 Very expensive

BROOKLYN BOWL

brooklynbowl.com/las-vegas
Nowhere on The Strip will you hear more rockin' indie music than at this hybrid bowling alley, restaurant and concert hall, with views of the High Roller wheel.

➕ D9 ✉ The LINQ Promenade, 3545 Las Vegas Boulevard South ☎ 702/862-2695
🕐 Daily 5pm–close (show times vary)
🚌 Harrah's/The LINQ 🚍 Deuce
💷 Expensive

TICKET INFORMATION

Popular long-running shows and new ones sell out quickly, so it's advisable to make reservations. Call the relevant hotel or check out its website, which will link to online ticket sales. Otherwise, shows can be reserved through TicketMaster (ticketmaster.com). Reservations are taken for long-running shows up to 30 or more days in advance; limited-time concerts or sporting events such as boxing matches can be reserved three months in advance. Note that shows can close with little notice so it is always best to check before you go to avoid disappointment.

CLEOPATRA'S BARGE

caesarspalace.com

This classic, floating red-and-gold club is a replica of the vessel that carried the Egyptian Queen Cleopatra. A DJ plays dance music during the week, and there's live music on weekends.

➕ C8–D8 ✉ Caesars Palace, 3570 Las Vegas Boulevard South ☎ 702/731-7333 ⏰ Tue–Thu 8pm–2am, Fri–Sat 8pm–3am 🚇 Flamingo/Caesars Palace 🚌 Deuce 💰 No cover charge

COLOSSEUM

caesarspalace.com

This magnificent auditorium has been purpose-built to stage extravaganzas and host international superstars. Céline Dion, Elton John and Mariah Carey have been among the star performers.

➕ C8–D8 ✉ Caesars Palace, 3570 Las Vegas Boulevard South ☎ 866/227-5938 ⏰ Daily (show times vary) 🚌 Deuce

COYOTE UGLY

coyoteuglysaloon.com/vegas

If you enjoyed the movie or have visited the New York original, you'll love the Las Vegas version. It's a fun Southern-style saloon with bartenders who dance on the bar.

➕ D10 ✉ New York New York, 3790 Las Vegas Boulevard South ☎ 702/740-6969 ⏰ Mon–Thu 6pm–3am, Fri–Sun 3pm–3am 🚇 MGM Grand 🚌 Deuce 💰 Cover charge: moderate

FLAMINGO LAS VEGAS

caesars.com/flamingo-las-vegas

Founded in the 1940s and formerly owned by Mob legend Bugsy Siegel, the Flamingo has long had a high reputation for hosting showbusiness legends—for example, Nat King Cole and Ella Fitzgerald once graced the stage here. Singing siblings Donny and Marie Osmond—still smiling broadly—were top of the bill for so long that a showroom was named after them. There are also stand-up comedians, magicians, drag artists and showgirls.

➕ D9 ✉ Flamingo, 3555 Las Vegas Boulevard South ☎ 702/777-2782 ⏰ Daily (show times vary) 🚇 Flamingo/Caesars Palace 🚌 Deuce 💰 Very expensive

Where there's a casino, there's a lounge or bar

GORDON BIERSCH

gordonbiersch.com
Exposed pipes and gleaming brewing equipment set the stage for this popular hangout. The beers include seasonally changing German brews, and the menu is crafted to suit the seasonal beers on tap.

🞤 F8 ✉ 3987 Paradise Road ☎ 702/312-5247 🕐 Sun–Thu 11am–11pm, Fri–Sat 11am–midnight 🚍 108

HAKKASAN

hakkasanlv.com
Attached to a double-decker Chinese restaurant, this three-level nightclub offers lounges, fine dining and dancing to the electronic sounds of superstar DJs, including Steve Aoki, Calvin Harris and Tiësto.

🞤 D10 ✉ MGM Grand, 3799 Las Vegas Boulevard South ☎ 702/891-3838 🕐 Wed–Sun 10.30pm–late 🚍 Deuce, SDX 🖐 Expensive

HOUSE OF BLUES

houseofblues.com/lasvegas
Bringing top musical acts to Las Vegas, this 1,500-seat venue is on three levels and features big-name stars, rock tribute bands and DJs in all musical genres. There's great food, including the popular Sunday Gospel Brunch buffet.

🞤 D11 ✉ Mandalay Bay, 3950 Las Vegas Boulevard South ☎ 702/632-7800 🕐 Daily (show times vary) 🚍 Deuce, SDX 🖐 Expensive–very expensive

INTRIGUE

intriguevegas.com
True to its name as one of the most enticing nightclubs in the city, Intrigue sets a standard for nightlife in Las Vegas. Sophisticated

jewel-tone and black combinations enhance intimate booth-style seating and the open-air dance floor extends toward a waterfall that cascades into a lagoon.

🞤 D7–E7 ✉ Wynn Las Vegas, 3131 Las Vegas Boulevard South ☎ 702/770-3000 🕐 Thu–Sat 10.30pm–4am 🚍 Deuce, SDX 🖐 Expensive

LAS VEGAS NATIONAL GOLF CLUB

lasvegasnational.com
Opened in 1961, this 18-hole golf course has glistening lakes. In 1996, Tiger Woods won his first PGA Tour victory here, and over the years the course has hosted many top-class tournaments.

🞤 J7–J8 ✉ 1911 East Desert Inn Road ☎ 702/889-1000 🕐 Daily (opening hours vary) 🚍 203 🖐 Very expensive

MANDALAY BAY EVENTS CENTER

mandalaybay.mgmresorts.com
This major venue seats 12,000 and hosts concerts and major sporting events. On some summer

CIRQUE DU SOLEIL

This troupe has taken circus arts to new levels with its breathtaking artistic concept shows. It has seven shows currently running, including *Mystère* at Treasure Island (Sat–Wed); *"O"* at Bellagio (Wed–Sun); *Zumanity* at New York New York (Fri–Tue); *KÀ* at MGM Grand (Tue–Wed); *The Beatles: LOVE* at The Mirage (▷ 129); and *Michael Jackson ONE* (▷ below), and its latest show, *R.U.N.*, at Luxor.

weekends, Mandalay Bay puts on big names at its artificial beach.
➕ D11 ✉ Mandalay Bay, 3950 Las Vegas Boulevard South ☎ 702/632-7777
🕐 Days and show times vary 🚇 Deuce, 203 💷 Very expensive

MARQUEE

marqueelasvegas.com
This vast entertainment venue is perfect for 24/7 clubbers. Groove till late in the nightclub's three-story space, or bask in the sun in one of the dayclub's infinity pools.
➕ D9 ✉ The Cosmopolitan of Las Vegas, 3708 Las Vegas Boulevard South
☎ 702/333-9000 🕐 Nightclub: Mon, Fri–Sat 10.30pm–4am; Dayclub: Apr–Oct daily 11.30am–sunset 🚇 Deuce 💷 Expensive

MGM GRAND GARDEN ARENA

mgmgrand.mgmresorts.com
This is one of the biggest venues in town, hosting events from top entertainers to world championship boxing. It seats 16,800 and tickets can be bought in advance.
➕ D10 ✉ MGM Grand, 3799 Las Vegas Boulevard South ☎ 702/531-3826
🕐 Days and show times vary 🚇 Deuce
💷 Expensive–very expensive

MICHAEL JACKSON ONE

cirquedusoleil.com
The King of Pop gets Cirque du Soleil's treatment in this tribute show, with a dramatic sequence of powerful, passionate and moving musical tableaux.

➕ D11 ✉ Mandalay Bay, 3950 Las Vegas Boulevard South ☎ 702/632-7580
🕐 Thu–Mon 7pm and 9.30pm 🚇 Deuce, SDX 💷 Very expensive

MINUS5 ICE BAR

minus5experience.com
Choose your venue—Mandalay Bay, The Venetian or The Linq Promenade—and then choose your package for the coolest attraction in town. Kids aged 7 to 15 are welcome at The Venetian and LINQ bars before 8pm.
➕ D11 ✉ Mandalay: 3377/3545/3930 Las Vegas Boulevard South ☎ 702/740-5800
🕐 11am–late 🚇 Deuce, SDX
💷 Moderate–expensive

NAPOLEON'S LOUNGE

caesars.com/paris-las-vegas
The French theme at this cocktail lounge incorporates more than 100 varieties of champagne and European-style appetizers. Note that if you sit near the dueling pianists you may become part of their comic routine.
➕ D9 ✉ Paris Las Vegas, 3655 Las Vegas Boulevard South ☎ 702/946-7000
🕐 Daily 5pm–1am 🚇 Deuce 💷 No cover charge

NATHAN BURTON COMEDY MAGIC

nathanburton.com
A former winner of *America's Got Talent*, showman Nathan Burton is an escapologist extraordinaire,

whose rapid-fire tricks include the wacky and slightly risqué, as well as artful improvisation. Expect plenty of dry ice, scantily clad showgirls and hilariously set-up audience members.

✉ D9 ✉ Saxe Theater, Miracle Mile Shops, 3663 Las Vegas Boulevard South ☎ 866/932-1818 🕐 Tue–Sun 4pm 🚍 Bally's/Paris Las Vegas 🚌 Deuce 💷 Very expensive

OMNIA

omnianightclub.com

This sumptuously sexy nightclub, inside Caesars Palace's casino, has three levels and an outdoor terrace, with great views over The Strip. Each room has its own DJ playing top electro and dance music. Look out for the spectacular centerpiece—a kinetic chandelier.

➕ C8–D8 ✉ Caesars Palace, 3570 Las Vegas Boulevard South ☎ 702/785-6200 🕐 Tue, Thu–Sun 10.30pm–4am 🚍 Flamingo/Caesars Palace 🚌 Deuce 💷 Expensive

Penn and Teller at the Rio

ORLEANS ARENA

orleansarena.com

This huge arena stages top concerts and a variety of sporting events, including NCAA basketball tournaments and motocross races. It has also hosted Disney on Ice.

➕ A10 ✉ Orleans, 4500 West Tropicana ☎ 800/745-3000 🕐 Days and show times vary 🚍 201 💷 Expensive–very expensive

PARASOL DOWN

wynnlasvegas.com

Sashay down the winding staircase from the glamorous casino floor to this whimsically designed cocktail lounge, where colorful parasols hang overhead. Tables have straight-ahead views of the resort's glassy Lake of Dreams, with its 40ft-high (12m) waterfall.

✉ D7–E7 ✉ Wynn Las Vegas, 3131 Las Vegas Boulevard South ☎ 702/770-7000 🕐 Daily noon–2am 🚌 Deuce, SDX 💷 No cover charge

THE PARK

theparkvegas.com

The Strip's newest outdoor entertainment, nightlife and dining complex revolves around the colorfully lit 40ft-high (12m) *Bliss Dance* sculpture. Major sporting events and concerts are held at T-Mobile Arena and Park Theater, where you can see stars such as Bruno Mars perform.

➕ D10 ✉ 3784 Las Vegas Boulevard South ☎ 702/693-7275 🕐 Daily (show times vary) 🚌 Deuce 💷 Admission free. Events: free–very expensive

PENN & TELLER

caesara.com/rio-las-vegas

This talented, eccentric partnership combines magic, illusions, juggling, comedy and stunts in an intelligent show. The pair have been together for more than 30 years: Penn is big, loud and talkative, while Teller is whimsically mute. Both stay on to meet fans after every show.

➕ B8 ✉ Rio, 3700 West Flamingo Road
☎ 702/777-2782 🕙 Sat–Wed 9pm
🚌 202 💲 Very expensive

PEPPERMILL FIRESIDE LOUNGE

peppermilllasvegas.com

Familiar from both the big and small screens, and the occasional music video, The Peppermill still boasts ankle-deep shag carpeting, fire pits, enormous white silk flowers and gushing indoor fountains as a tribute to vintage Vegas.

➕ E7 ✉ 2985 Las Vegas Boulevard South
☎ 702/735-4177 🕙 Daily 24 hours
🚌 Deuce, SDX 💲 No cover charge

ROYAL LINKS GOLF CLUB

royallinksgolfclub.com

This course has holes based on those from famous British Open courses, including St. Andrews, Royal Troon, Carnoustie and Turnberry. The 18th hole looks like a medieval castle.

➕ Off map ✉ 5995 East Vegas Valley Drive, 8 miles (13km) east of The Strip
☎ 702/765-0484 🕙 Daily (opening hours vary) 🚌 SDX 💲 Very expensive

SKYFALL LOUNGE

delanolasvegas.mgmresorts.com

Mix good music, savvy DJs, great cocktails, an innovative bar menu, tasty tapas and views from 64 floors up and you have one of The Strip's most fashionable spots. Reserve a table indoors or go out on the balcony.

➕ D11 ✉ Delano Las Vegas at Mandalay Bay, 3940 Las Vegas Boulevard South ☎ 877/632-5450 🕙 Sun–Thu 5pm–midnight, Fri–Sat 5pm–1am
🚌 Deuce, SDX 💲 Usually no cover charge

SPEED VEGAS

speedvegas.com

Drive a supercar such as a Ferrari or Lamborghini at this high-speed city race track, or take to an off-road vehicle or trophy truck on a dirt or desert road for an exhilarating experience with jumps, turns and ramps.

➕ Off map ✉ 14200 Las Vegas Boulevard South ☎ 702/213-9068 🕙 Daily 8am–6pm 🚌 Shuttle buses from resorts
💲 Expensive

THOMAS & MACK CENTER

thomasandmack.com

This state-of-the-art, multipurpose arena, seating 19,500, stages world-class entertainment and major events, from monster-truck racing, boxing and rodeos to concerts, basketball and ice shows.

➕ G10 ✉ University of Nevada, Las Vegas (UNLV), 4505 South Maryland Parkway
☎ 702/739-3267 🕙 Days and show times vary 🚌 108 💲 Expensive–very expensive

UNLV ARTS CENTER

pac.unlv.edu

See major international artists perform classical and popular music, dance, theater, ballet and opera. The center comprises the Artemus W. Ham Concert Hall, home to symphony orchestra and chamber music recitals, and the Judy Bayley Theatre.

🔳 G9 ✉ University of Nevada, Las Vegas (UNLV), 4505 South Maryland Parkway ☎ 702/895-3011 🕐 Days and show times vary 🚌 109 💲 Expensive–very expensive

V THEATER

vtheaterboxoffice.com

This specially tailored venue, next door to Planet Hollywood, showcases a varied program during the day and evening, from comedy, variety and magic to game shows and tribute acts.

🔳 D9 ✉ Miracle Mile Shops, 3663 Las Vegas Boulevard South ☎ 866/932-1818 🕐 Daily (show times vary) 🚌 Deuce 💲 Expensive–very expensive

VEGAS INDOOR SKYDIVING

vegasindoorskydiving.com

Test your skills at this exciting sporting challenge. A vertical wind tunnel simulates an authentic free-fall experience of skydiving in a column of air, with vertical air-speeds of up to 120mph (193kph). No experience is needed though there are some maximum weight limits and other restrictions to consider.

🔳 E7 ✉ 200 Convention Center Drive ☎ 702/731-4768 🕐 Daily 9.30–8 🚌 108, Deuce, SDX 💲 Expensive

WESTGATE LAS VEGAS RESORT & CASINO

westgateresorts.com

A variety of talented musicians, comedians and magicians perform here. Formerly the Las Vegas Hilton, where Elvis staged a comeback in 1976, it stages big acts at the International Westgate Theater and smaller comedy and magic shows, showgirl revues and live music in the Westgate Cabaret.

🔳 F7 ✉ 3000 Paradise Road ☎ 702/732-5111 🕐 Days and show times vary 🚌 Las Vegas Convention Center 🚌 108 💲 Expensive–very expensive

XS

xslasvegas.com

After dark on The Strip, you'll find the most fashionable crowd in Las Vegas poolside at the Encore Beach Club. On some hot, sultry Sunday evenings during summer, come for "nightswim" pool parties. Dress to impress, no jeans.

🔳 E7 ✉ Encore at Wynn Las Vegas, 3131 Las Vegas Boulevard South ☎ 702/770-7300 🕐 Fri–Mon 10pm–4am 🚌 Deuce, SDX 💲 Expensive

Simulated skydiving in a wind tunnel

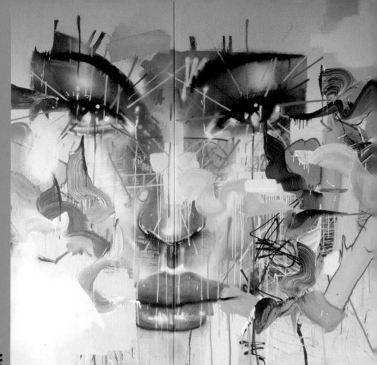

Eat

There are places to eat across the city to suit all tastes and budgets. In this section, establishments are listed alphabetically.

EAT

Introduction

In the last decade, the dining scene in Las Vegas has heated up, especially with the arrival of world-famous chefs and celebrity restaurant owners on The Strip.

So What's on Offer?
The famous Vegas buffet has become much more exciting and provides something for everyone at a reasonable price. There are endless top-class establishments where you can feast on the superb cuisine of Michelin-star chefs, and there's also the opportunity to dine at a restaurant run by a celebrity chef. The sheer variety of cuisine is astonishing, from fine French, Italian and Chinese to Mediterranean, Thai/Korean fusion and Pacific Rim. All-night casino coffee shops still play an important role, as do traditional steak houses.

Dining Tips
It can be hard to get a table at high-end restaurants, especially on Friday and Saturday nights. Plan ahead—you can reserve up to 30 days or more in advance. Many of these open for dinner only. Mid-range eateries are more likely to be open all day, and you will likely not need a reservation for breakfast or lunch. Most major hotels have a fast-food court to grab a quick bite, and many have a buffet open for breakfast, lunch and dinner. Buffet lines can be long, so allow plenty of time.

DINNER SHOWS

Take advantage of one of the dinner shows on offer, where you can eat and be thoroughly entertained at the same time. Probably the most popular of these for families is the Tournament of Kings at the Excalibur (▷ 68), where your meal is accompanied by a jousting tournament, dragons, wizards and great special effects. Many other casinos on The Strip offer special pre-show dinner menus, including at restaurants at Bellagio, Caesars Palace, MGM Grand and Wynn Las Vegas.

From top: All types of food are on offer around the clock; the Lago Bar at the Bellagio; a café on the replica of St. Mark's Square; Joël Robuchon's restaurant

Directory

SOUTH STRIP
Buffets
Bayside Buffet
Cafés, Pubs and Lounges
Il Fornaio Panetteria & Restaurant
Veranda Bar
European
Jaleo
Joël Robuchon
Red Square
International
Fleur
Mexican
Border Grill
Modern American
Aureole
Steaks and Seafood
Charlie Palmer Steak
Craftsteak
Emeril's New Orleans Fish House

CENTER STRIP
Asian/Fusion
China Poblano
Koi
Momofuku
Nobu
Buffets
Bacchanal Buffet
The Buffet
Carnival World Buffet
Wicked Spoon
Cafés, Pubs and Lounges
Gordon Ramsay Pub & Grill
Hash House a Go Go
Holsteins Shakes and Buns
Jean Philippe Patisserie
Maxies
Yardbird Southern Table & Bar
French
Bouchon
Mon Ami Gabi
Picasso
Italian
Battista's Hole in the Wall
Canaletto
GIADA

Lago
Rao's
Mexican/Southwestern
Mesa Grill
Steaks and Seafood
Lawry's The Prime Rib
Michael Mina
Pampas Brazilian Grille
Smith & Wollensky
Strip House

NORTH STRIP
Asian/Fusion
Lotus of Siam
RA Sushi
Sparrow & Wolf
European
Top of the World
Italian
Piero's
North American and Mexican
Johnny Rocket's
Steaks and Seafood
ENVY the Steakhouse
THE Steak House

DOWNTOWN
American
Carson Kitchen
Asian/Fusion
Lillie's Asian Cuisine
Second Street Grill
Buffets
Garden Court Buffet
Cafés
Binion's Café
European
Hugo's Cellar
Mexican
Doña Maria Tamales
Steaks and Seafood
Top of Binion's Steakhouse
Triple George Grill

Eating A–Z

AUREOLE $$$

mandalaybay.mgmresorts.com
Renowned chef Charlie Palmer's restaurant has big windows, glass-covered views of waterfalls and a massive award-winning wine tower, which holds more than 3,200 bottles. American-style meat and seafood dishes dominate the first-class, seasonally changing menu here.

➕ D11 ✉ Mandalay Bay, 3950 Las Vegas Boulevard South ☎ 702/632-7401 ⏰ Mon–Sat 5.30–10.30pm 🚌 Deuce, SDX

BACCHANAL BUFFET $$

caesars.com/caesars-palace
The Strip's most expensive casino buffet is the reigning champion when it comes to satisfying all-you-can-eat feasts with more than 500 dishes. The huge refurbished dining space looks out onto the Garden of the Gods.

➕ C8–D8 ✉ Caesars Palace, 3570 Las Vegas Boulevard South ☎ 702/732-7928 ⏰ Daily 7.30am–10pm 🚊 Flamingo/Caesars Palace 🚌 Deuce

BATTISTA'S HOLE IN THE WALL $$

battistaslasvegas.com
For more than 50 years, tourists and locals alike have been flocking here for the excellent Italian-American comfort food, served with heart-warming style.

➕ D9 ✉ 4041 LINQ Lane ☎ 702/732-1424 ⏰ Daily 5–10.30pm 🚊 Flamingo/Caesars Palace 🚌 Deuce, SDX

BAYSIDE BUFFET $$

mandalaybay.mgmresorts.com
Floor-to-ceiling windows give sweeping views of the tropical lagoon outside. Although the buffet is not over-large, the cuisine is very good, with excellent salads, hearty meats and one of The Strip's better dessert selections, all made on the premises.

➕ D11 ✉ Mandalay Bay, 3950 Las Vegas Boulevard South ☎ 702/632-7200 ⏰ Daily 7–2.30, 4.45–9.45 🚌 Deuce, SDX

BINION'S CAFÉ $

binions.com
If you're looking for a great place for a light snack or something more substantial at a low price, try this simple no-frills café. The breakfasts are particularly good.

➕ G3 ✉ Binion's, 128 East Fremont Street ☎ 702/382-1600 ⏰ Daily 7am–2am 🚌 Deuce, SDX

BORDER GRILL $$

bordergrill.mgmresorts.com
Come here for great Mexican cooking and California-influenced fusion tastes in a lively, colorful setting. Lunch on TV chefs Susan Feniger and Mary Sue Milliken's creations on the patio or get a take-out taco.

➕ D11 ✉ Mandalay Bay, 3950 Las Vegas Boulevard South ☎ 702/632-7200 ⏰ Mon–Fri 11–10, Sat 10am–11pm, Sun 10–10 🚌 Deuce, SDX

BOUCHON $$

venetian.com/restaurants/bouchon
World-renowned chef Thomas Keller showcases his French bistro

EAT

fare at Bouchon, located in the Venezia Tower. Dark wooden seating, antique lights, a mosaic tile floor and hand-painted murals provide a café-style ambience amid a poolside garden.

🔲 D8 ✉ The Venetian, 3355 Las Vegas Boulevard South ☎ 702/414-6200 🕐 Mon–Fri 7am–1pm, Sat–Sun 7am–2pm, daily 5–10pm 🚌 Deuce

THE BUFFET $$

bellagio.mgmresorts.com

This is one of the best-known buffets on The Strip. It offers many different types of cuisine, including Italian and Asian in a European marketplace-style setting.

🔲 C9–D9 ✉ Bellagio, 3600 Las Vegas Boulevard South ☎ 702/693-7111 🕐 Daily 7am–10pm 🚌 Deuce, SDX

CANALETTO $$

ilfornaio.com/canalettolasvegas

Where better to sample northern Italian cuisine than on a re-creation of Venice's St. Mark's Square? Some little-known Italian wines are on offer to complement choices such as wood-fired pizza, saffron risotto or tagliatelle pasta with brandy cream sauce.

🔲 D8 ✉ Grand Canal Shoppes, 3377 Las Vegas Boulevard South ☎ 702/733-0070 🕐 Sun–Thu 11–11, Fri–Sat 11–midnight 🚌 Deuce

CARNIVAL WORLD BUFFET $$

caesars.com/rio-las-vegas

This is one of the best buffets in Las Vegas, with chefs cooking on view at various points around the serving islands. There are almost a dozen styles of cuisine on offer, from Italian gelato to Asian barbecue. Fresh seafood is the house specialty.

🔲 B8 ✉ Rio All-Suite Hotel & Casino, 3700 West Flamingo Road ☎ 702/777-7757 🕐 Mon–Thu 4–9pm, Fri 4–9.30pm, Sat–Sun 9am–9.30pm 🚌 202

CARSON KITCHEN $$

carsonkitchen.com

Gourmet burgers, a rooftop patio and very good cocktails are the main draw here. Expect a simple interior (many of the seats are bar stools) and buzzing atmosphere at this intimate venue, which is just around the corner from the Fremont Street Experience.

🔲 G3 ✉ 124 South 6th Street, Suite 100 ☎ 702/473-9523 🕐 Sun–Wed 11.30–10, Thu–Sat 11.30–11 🚌 Deuce, SDX

CHARLIE PALMER STEAK $$$

charliepalmer.com

Gleaming woodwork and leather banquettes set the scene for self-styled "progessive American cooking." A meal here might include charcoal-grilled filet mignon, a porterhouse steak for two with truffled potato gratin or steamed halibut.

🔲 D11 ✉ Four Seasons, 3960 Las Vegas Boulevard South ☎ 702/632-5120 🕐 Mon–Sat 5–10.30pm 🚌 Deuce, SDX

CHINA POBLANO $$

chinapoblano.com

East meets West here, with a menu offering some of the best-known dishes from Mexico and China—separate, not fusion—in a colorful, smart setting. Choose from tacos, dim sum, noodles, ceviche and more. The cocktails are imaginative.

🔲 D9 ✉ The Cosmopolitan, 3708 Las Vegas Boulevard South, Level 2 ☎ 702/698-7900 🕐 Sun–Thu 11.30–11, Fri–Sat 11.30–11.30 🚌 Deuce

CRAFTSTEAK $$$

craftsteaklasvegas.com

Hand-selected beef from small farms and artisan producers is served here, with the magic touch of award-winning chef Tom Colicchio. The vegetable sides are not an afterthought here: sample garlicky heirloom cauliflower or butternut squash with nut streusel.

🔁 D10 ⊠ MGM Grand, 3799 Las Vegas Boulevard South ☎ 702/891-7318 ⏰ Daily 5.30–10.30pm 🚉 MGM Grand 🚌 Deuce, SDX

DOÑA MARIA TAMALES $

donamariatamales.com

The tamales at this Mexican restaurant are great. Choose from shredded chicken in spicy green sauce, Monterey Jack cheese with green chilies or pork in red sauce, all wrapped in cornmeal.

🔁 G4 ⊠ 910 Las Vegas Boulevard South ☎ 702/382-6538 ⏰ Daily 8am–10pm 🚌 Deuce, SDX

EMERIL'S NEW ORLEANS FISH HOUSE $$$

emerilsrestaurants.com

This is a scaled-down re-creation of Emeril Lagasse's New Orleans restaurant, specializing in spicy Creole/Cajun recipes. The menu includes barbecued shrimp, jumbo crab cakes, fried frog legs, Louisiana-style broiled oysters and sumptuous banana cream pie drizzled with caramel.

🔁 D10 ⊠ MGM Grand, 3799 Las Vegas Boulevard South ☎ 702/891-7374 ⏰ Daily 11.30–10 🚌 Deuce, SDX

ENVY THE STEAKHOUSE $$$

marriott.com

In this svelte dining room near the convention center, top-quality fresh ingredients appear in innovative dishes, redefining the usual steak-house offerings. Soothing red shades give a sophisticated feel. It's also popular for power breakfasts.

🔁 F7 ⊠ Renaissance, 3400 Paradise Road ☎ 702/784-5716 ⏰ Daily 6.30–11, 5–10 🚉 Las Vegas Convention Center 🚌 108

FLEUR $$$

hubertkeller.com

Celebrity chef Hubert Keller serves bold, French fusion cuisine. Nibble on Parmesan paprika popcorn or blow your budget on the $5,000 FleurBurger: wagyu minced beef, foie gras and truffles, washed down with 1995 Chateau Petrus. The small tapas-style dishes are ideal for sharing.

🔁 D11 ⊠ Mandalay Bay, 3950 Las Vegas Boulevard South ☎ 702/632-7200 ⏰ Daily 11–4, 5.30–10 🚌 Deuce, SDX

GARDEN COURT BUFFET $

mainstreetcasino.com

Watch your food being prepared for you at what is one of Downtown's best buffets. Choices include Mexican, Asian and American, and there are specialty nights such as seafood dinners on

Friday or prime rib and scampi on Saturday evenings.

➕ G2 ✉ Main Street Station, 200 North Main Street ☎ 702/387-1896 🕐 Sun–Thu 7am–9pm, Fri–Sat 7am–10pm 🚌 Deuce, SDX

GIADA $$$

giadadelaurentiis.com/vegas

TV celebrity chef Giada de Laurentiis personally oversees the menu at this light-filled dining room hung with vintage Italian cinema posters. House-made Italian antipasti and salumi are always good bets, as is the lemon-pesto grilled cheese sandwich at weekend brunch.

➕ D9 ✉ The Cromwell, 3595 Las Vegas Boulevard South ☎ 855/442-3271 🕐 Daily 5–10.30pm, brunch Fri–Sat 9am–3pm 🚇 Flamingo/Caesars Palace 🚌 Deuce

GORDON RAMSAY PUB & GRILL $$

gordonramsayrestaurants.com

The notoriously no-nonsense British chef introduces Vegas to the culinary delights of the British pub, with two connected restaurants offering traditional dishes, including fish and chips and shepherd's pie, plus a wide choice of beers.

➕ C8–D8 ✉ Caesars Palace, 3570 Las Vegas Boulevard South ☎ 702/731-7410 🕐 Sun–Thu 11–11, Fri–Sat 11am–midnight 🚇 Flamingo/Caesars Palace 🚌 Deuce

HASH HOUSE A GO GO $$

hashhouseagogo.com/vegas

Plates of farm food with a twist are so huge that you'll feel full for the day. Sage fried chicken over waffles, corned beef hash and bloody Marys are all brunch favorites.

➕ D8–D9 ✉ The LINQ Hotel & Casino, 3535 Las Vegas Boulevard South ☎ 702/254-4646 🕐 Daily 24 hours 🚇 Harrah's/The LINQ 🚌 Deuce

HOLSTEINS SHAKES AND BUNS $$

holsteinsburgers.com/lasvegas

One of The Strip's most popular burger bars, Holsteins dishes up towering stacks of fried onion rings and deluxe burgers. Pair your burger with "bamboozled" milkshakes spiked with liqueurs, flavored vodkas and nostalgic candy, or go for an American craft beer.

➕ D9 ✉ The Cosmopolitan of Las Vegas, 3708 Las Vegas Boulevard South ☎ 702/698-7940 🕐 Mon–Thu 11am–midnight, Fri–Sat 11am–1am, Sun 9am–midnight 🚌 Deuce

HUGO'S CELLAR $$$

hugoscellar.com

Below street level, this romantic restaurant has a touch of old-school class. Each woman receives a red rose as she enters the low-lit, dark-wood space. There's excellent Continental cuisine and some dishes are prepared at the table.

➕ G3 ✉ Four Queens, 202 Fremont Street ☎ 702/385-4011 🕐 Daily 5–10pm 🚌 Deuce, SDX

BUFFET KNOW-HOW

Buffets offer breakfast, lunch and dinner. They are a great option for families because there is sure to be something for everyone. Buffets also offer value for money. This does, of course, mean that they are popular and lines can be long, especially at peak times. At the most popular buffets, you may need to allow up to two to three hours for your meal.

IL FORNAIO PANETTERIA & RESTAURANT $–$$

ilfornaio.com/lasvegas

It's worth making a special trip to this Italian bakery café just for its espresso-mocha scones with chocolate chunks. Italian-American breakfasts, lunches and dinners are served in the restaurant.

➕ D10 ✉ New York New York, 3790 Las Vegas Boulevard South ☎ 702/650-6500 🕐 Panetteria: daily 6am–5.30pm. Restaurant: Sun–Thu 7.30am–11pm, Fri–Sat 7.30am–midnight 🚊 MGM Grand 🚌 Deuce, SDX

JALEO $$

jaleo.com

Celebrity master chef José Andrés brings the best of Spanish cuisine to Vegas. Besides the delectable tapas snacks, try Jaleo's Ibérico-cured Spanish ham, or its classic paella, cooked over a wood fire.

➕ D9 ✉ The Cosmopolitan of Las Vegas, 3708 Las Vegas Boulevard South ☎ 702/698-7950 🕐 Sun–Thu noon–11pm, Fri–Sat noon–midnight 🚌 Deuce

JOËL ROBUCHON $$$

mgmgrand.com

Robuchon's reputation for the highest standards is upheld in the sophisticated 16-course fine French menu or, if you prefer a scaled-down version, choose the four-course tasting menu.

➕ D10 ✉ MGM Grand, 3799 Las Vegas Boulevard South ☎ 702/891-7925 🕐 Daily 5.30–10pm 🚊 MGM Grand 🚌 Deuce, SDX

JOHNNY ROCKETS $

johnnyrockets.com

The servers at this American retro diner, which serves burgers, tasty fries, club sandwiches, great malts and shakes, wear outfits straight out of a 1950s soda fountain. It's kid-friendly and conveniently located for shopaholic families.

➕ D7 ✉ Fashion Show, 3200 Las Vegas Boulevard South ☎ 702/784-0107 🕐 Mon–Sat 9–9, Sun 11–7 🚌 Deuce, SDX

KOI $$$

koirestaurant.com

This outpost of the famous New York hotspot exudes a sophisticated tone, with the best views of Bellagio's fountains. Koi cooks up modern and traditional Japanese-inspired dishes with a Californian accent; try the Kobe beef carpaccio with fried shiitake mushrooms.

➕ D9 ✉ Planet Hollywood, 3667 Las Vegas Boulevard South ☎ 702/454-4555 🕐 Sun–Thu 5.30–10.30pm, Fri–Sat 5.30–11.30pm 🚌 Deuce

LAGO $$

bellagio.com/lago

From talented chef Julian Serrano, this sleek lakeside dining room

---

EATING ON A BUDGET

If you are on a budget you have several options for eating inexpensively. So long as you keep playing, most casinos will ply you with free food and drink—though take care not to spend more than you save. There are plenty of well-known fast-food chains on The Strip, if all you want is to refuel on the go. Try the various food courts inside casinos and shopping malls on The Strip and beyond, such as Las Vegas Chinatown Plaza (▷ 119). Many informal restaurants, such as the Peppermill (▷ 134), serve large portions, and are happy to provide take-out containers for leftovers.

at Bellagio offers modern Italian cuisine with an artistic touch. Come for three-course tasting menus at lunch or Sunday brunches with house-made pastry baskets and tiramisu for dessert.

✚ C9–D9 ✉ Bellagio, 3600 Las Vegas Boulevard South ☎ 702/693-8865 🕙 Mon–Thu 11.30am–11pm, Fri–Sat 11.30am–midnight, Sun 10.30am–11pm 🚌 Deuce, SDX

LAWRY'S THE PRIME RIB $$$

lawrysonline.com

Lawry's is popular for its perfectly cooked, tasty prime rib. Servers in stylish uniforms and starched white caps tend to your every need in the art deco surroundings.

✚ E9 ✉ 4043 Howard Hughes Parkway ☎ 702/893-2223 🕙 Mon–Fri 11.30–2, 5–10pm, Sat 5–10pm, Sun 4–9pm 🚌 202

LILLIE'S ASIAN CUISINE $$

goldennugget.com

There's an eclectic mix of cuisines here, but the menu is mostly Chinese with good-quality Sichuan and Cantonese dishes, plus Japanese dishes served on hibachi hot griddles.

✚ G3 ✉ Golden Nugget, 129 East Fremont Street ☎ 702/386-8131 🕙 Daily 5pm–midnight 🚌 Deuce, SDX

LOTUS OF SIAM $

lotusofsiamlv.com

Lotus of Siam is one of the top Thai restaurants in Las Vegas, with a huge menu of authentic dishes. Let them know how hot you like your food and, if you overdo it, cool down with the coconut ice cream for dessert.

✚ G6 ✉ 953 East Sahara Avenue ☎ 702/735-3033 🕙 Mon–Fri 11.30–2.30, daily 5.30–10pm 🚌 SDX

Mon Ami Gabi

MAXIES $

maxieslv.com

This relaxed restaurant right at the base of the High Roller has a simple menu of treats, with all-day breakfast, deli dishes and burgers the most popular. The lolly-waffles and elaborate milkshakes are also a big draw. Eat in the relaxed interior or get something from the "grab and go" menu.

✚ D8 ✉ 3545 Las Vegas Boulevard South ☎ 702/754-4400 🕙 Daily 8am–10pm 🚌 Flamingo/Caesars Palace 🚌 Deuce

MESA GRILL $$$

caesars.com

Sample modern US Southwestern-Mexican fusion cuisine from celebrity chef Bobby Flay, whose specialties include ancho chile and honey-glazed salmon and blue corn lobster tacos. The fruit margaritas and Blue Agave tequilas will leave you glowing.

✚ C8–D8 ✉ Caesars Palace, 3570 Las Vegas Boulevard South ☎ 702/731-7731 🕙 Mon–Fri 11–2.30, 5–11, Sat–Sun 10.30–3, 5–11 🚌 Flamingo/Caesars Palace 🚌 Deuce

MICHAEL MINA $$$

michaelmina.net

Enjoy seafood favorites that chef Michael Mina has made famous with his daring approach, using unexpected flavors and textures blended with Mediterranean and Californian ingredients. Sleek, yet casual, this is the perfect place to try Mina's signature dishes.

🔢 C9–D9 ✉ Bellagio, 3600 Las Vegas Boulevard South ☎ 702/693-7225 🕐 Mon–Sat 5.30–10pm 🚍 Deuce, SDX

MOMOFUKU $$$

vegas.momofuku.com

Renegade New York City chef David Chang has brought his game-changing cuisine to The Strip. Feast on dishes showing American, Korean and Japanese influences, such as black truffle ramen, roasted beets with XO sauce or puffy shrimp buns with spicy mayo.

🔢 D9 ✉ The Cosmopolitan of Las Vegas, 3708 Las Vegas Boulevard South ☎ 702/698-2663 🕐 Daily 11am–2pm, 5.30–11pm 🚍 Deuce

MON AMI GABI $$

monamigabi.com

Fine French fare is served in the sunlit atrium or on the patio under the faux Eiffel Tower. Tables are set beneath sparkling lights, with a great view of the Bellagio's famous fountain show.

🔢 D9 ✉ Paris Las Vegas, 3655 Las Vegas Boulevard South ☎ 702/944-4224 🕐 Daily 7am–11pm 🚇 Bally's/Paris 🚍 Deuce, SDX

NOBU $$$

noburestaurants.com

This is the largest of the popular Japanese-fusion restaurants. Specialties include black cod with miso, or try the blow-out multi-course *omakase*-tasting menu, created daily in chef Matsuhisa's signature culinary style.

🔢 C8–D8 ✉ Caesars Palace, 3570 Las Vegas Boulevard South ☎ 702/785-6674 🕐 Sun–Thu 5–11pm, Fri–Sat 5pm–midnight 🚇 Flamingo/Caesars Palace 🚍 Deuce

PAMPAS BRAZILIAN GRILLE $$$

pampasusa.com

Come here to enjoy an authentic taste of Brazil. Helpful servers bring sizzling skewers of the finest meats to your table in an endless parade while you feast on mountains of fresh salads, soups, vegetables and desserts at the appetizing buffet.

🔢 D9 ✉ Miracle Mile Shops, 3663 Las Vegas Boulevard South ☎ 702/737-4748 🕐 Sun–Thu 8.30am–10.30pm, Fri–Sat 9am–11.30pm 🚍 Deuce

PICASSO $$$

bellagiolasvegas.com

This is among the most highly rated restaurants in Vegas. The refined cuisine reflects places in which the artist lived (south of France and Spain), and there are more than 1,500 bottles of the finest European wine. The Picassos on the walls are authentic.

DINING WITH A VIEW

There are some wonderful spots in Vegas where you can savor great views while you eat, but one of the best is the Top of the World restaurant (▷ 149). On the 106th floor of the Stratosphere Tower, it makes one revolution in 60 minutes, during which you can see The Strip, the mountains, the valleys and beyond. Also try Mon Ami Gabi (▷ above).

C9–D9 Bellagio, 3600 Las Vegas Boulevard South 702/693-8865 Wed–Mon 5.30–9.30pm Deuce, SDX

PIERO'S $$$

pieroscuisine.com

Sublime Italian cuisine is served at Piero's, one of the city's oldest established restaurants. Former patrons include Michael Jordan, Arnold Schwarzenegger and Keith Richards. Osso bucco, one of Piero's signature dishes, melts in the mouth, and the fish and seafood are also excellent.

E7 335 Convention Center Drive 702/369-2305 Daily 5.30–10pm 108

RA SUSHI $$

rasushi.com

An upbeat, casual mood is the perfect setting to enjoy fresh sushi, Japanese-fusion cuisine and signature dishes so good that you'll want to return. Bright wall hangings and globe lighting provide accents.

D7–D8 Fashion Show, 3200 Las Vegas Boulevard South 702/696-0008 Sun–Thu 11am–midnight, Fri–Sat 11am–1am Deuce, SDX

RAO'S $$$

raosrestaurants.com

This highly rated family-run Italian restaurant from New York City serves traditional dishes, using the best ingredients. Try the giant house-made meatballs in marinara sauce, the osso bucco or Uncle Vincent's succulent lemon chicken.

C8–D8 Caesars Palace, 3570 Las Vegas Boulevard South 702/731-7267 Sun–Thu 4.30–10pm, Fri–Sat 4.30–10.30pm Flamingo/Caesars Palace Deuce

---

> ### JUST DESSERTS
>
> If you're after dessert then head to Jean Philippe Patisserie at Aria (▷ 153) or the Bellagio (▷ 14–15) for pastries, eclairs and cookies. At The Venetian (▷ 58–59), Bouchon Bakery also has pastries and cookies, as does Payard Patisserie inside Caesars Palace (▷ 16–17).

RED SQUARE $$$

mandalaybay.mgmresorts.com

Wash latkes and blinis down with vodka at the ice-topped bar, or choose US and Italian dishes in this Russian-theme restaurant, where the headless statue of Lenin, the red-velvet drapes and the fake communist propaganda give the game away.

D11 Mandalay Bay, 3950 Las Vegas Boulevard South 702/632-7200 Sun–Thu 4–10pm, Fri–Sat 4–11pm Flamingo/Caesars Palace Deuce, SDX

SECOND STREET GRILL $$

fremontcasino.com

Step back in time at this hidden gem and sample good Pacific Rim and contemporary cuisine at affordable prices. Soft lighting and rich woods encourage you to relax in the oversized banquettes.

G3 Fremont Casino, 200 Fremont Street 702/385-3232 Sun–Mon, Thu 5–10pm, Fri–Sat 5–11pm Deuce, SDX

SMITH & WOLLENSKY $$$

smithandwollensky.com

One of the most talked-about restaurant openings in the city in recent years, this upscale steakhouse, which covers two stories, also serves seafood. Dine in the cozy lounge, pick a seat with a view of the butcher room, or go for

EAT

the private room overlooking the promenade. There's an extensive cocktail and drinks menu to match your meal.

🔶 D8 ✉ 3377 Las Vegas Boulevard South (The Grand Canal Shoppes) ☎ 702/637-1515 🕐 Sun–Thu 11.30–10.30, Fri, Sat 11.30am–midnight 🚌 Deuce

SPARROW AND WOLF $$

sparrowandwolflv.com

"Diverse–Coexist–Provide" is the mantra of this intimate, stand-out restaurant, which showcases cuisine from a mix of neighborhoods. The weekly changing menu is as exciting as its craft beer and cocktail list. Booking is essential.

🔶 A7 ✉ 4480 Spring Mountain Road, Suite 100 ☎ 702/790-2147 🕐 Daily 5–10pm 🚌 Spring Mountain@Arville (W)

THE STEAK HOUSE $$$

circuscircus.mgmresorts.com

This old-timer eastery is popular for its prime ribs and mesquite charcoal-grilled Midwestern steaks at reasonable prices. Seafood, lobster, chicken and lamb are also on the menu, and all can be enjoyed with side dishes such as baked potatoes and green salads.

🔶 E6 ✉ Circus Circus, 2880 Las Vegas Boulevard South ☎ 702/794-3767 🕐 Sun–Fri 4–10pm, Sat 4–11pm 🚌 Deuce

STRIP HOUSE $$$

striphouse.com

Excellent American cuisine is served in this intimate restaurant, whose walls are lined with retro black-and-white portraits of pin-up models. The steaks are for serious carnivores, going up to the massive 20oz (565g) New York Strip. There's also an impressive rare scotch menu.

🔶 D9 ✉ Planet Hollywood, 3667 Las Vegas Boulevard South ☎ 702/737-5200 🕐 Sun–Wed 5–10pm, Thu–Sat 5–11pm 🚌 Deuce

TOP OF BINION'S STEAKHOUSE $$$

binions.com

Settle down to delicious succulent steaks and chops (although there

Dining at the Stratosphere Tower's Top of the World revolving restaurant

are vegan options too) while taking in the spectacular views of Las Vegas from the 24th floor. The vibe is vintage Vegas, with a crowd of die-hard gamblers, cowboys wearing Stetson hats and tourists.

🔢 G3 ✉ Binion's, 128 Fremont Street ☎ 702/382-1600 ⏰ Daily 5–10pm 🚌 Deuce, SDX

TOP OF THE WORLD $$$

topoftheworldlv.com

Master chefs Rick Giffen and Claude Gaty have achieved the seemingly impossible at this stylish revolving restaurant: to upstage the best view in the city. The menu gives traditional French cuisine flavor-packed Asian twists, such as crab cakes with ginger slaw, or try the tasting menu.

🔢 E5–F5 ✉ Stratosphere Tower, 2000 Las Vegas Boulevard South ☎ 702/380-7711 ⏰ Daily 11–11 🚌 Deuce

TRIPLE GEORGE GRILL $$–$$$

triplegeorgegrill.com

This sophisticated Downtown grill offers reliable steaks and chops, fine seafood dishes, fantastic desserts and serious cocktails. Portions are big so you may want to share a main course.

🔢 G3 ✉ 201 North Third Street ☎ 702/384-2761 ⏰ Mon–Thu 11–11, Fri 11am–midnight, Sat 4–midnight, Sun 4–11 🚌 Deuce

VERANDA BAR $$

fourseasons.com/lasvegas

Bright and airy in the daytime, low lit and intimate after dark, this elegant but casual snack and cocktail bar offers a wide range of tasty Italian antipasti and light dishes, which are ideal for a quick bite before a show. There's even an afternoon tea option of delicate sandwiches and pastries.

🔢 D11 ✉ Four Seasons, 3960 Las Vegas Boulevard South ☎ 702/632-5000 ⏰ Daily 11–10 🚌 Deuce

WICKED SPOON $$

cosmopolitanlasvegas.com

The tiny plates let hungry diners cram even more onto their trays at this elevated Vegas buffet. The dessert area offers endless choices, and more than a dozen hot-food stations have options not easily found elsewhere, such as bone marrow and paella.

🔢 D9 ✉ The Cosmopolitan of Las Vegas, 3708 Las Vegas Boulevard South ☎ 877/893-2001 ⏰ Mon–Thu 8am–9pm, Fri–Sat 8am–10pm, Sun 8am–9pm 🚌 Deuce

YARDBIRD SOUTHERN TABLE & BAR $$

runchickenrun.com

Scratch an itch for good, ol' Southern favorites like buttermilk fried chicken, BBQ pork ribs, okra and fluffy biscuits at this laid-back dining lounge. Inventive cocktails in mason jars and a long list of bourbons and craft beers are kept on hand.

🔢 D8 ✉ Grand Canal Shoppes, 3355 Las Vegas Boulevard South ☎ 702/297-6541 🈳 Mon–Thu 11–11, Fri 11am–midnight, Sat 10am–midnight, Sun 10am–11pm 🚌 Deuce

EAT

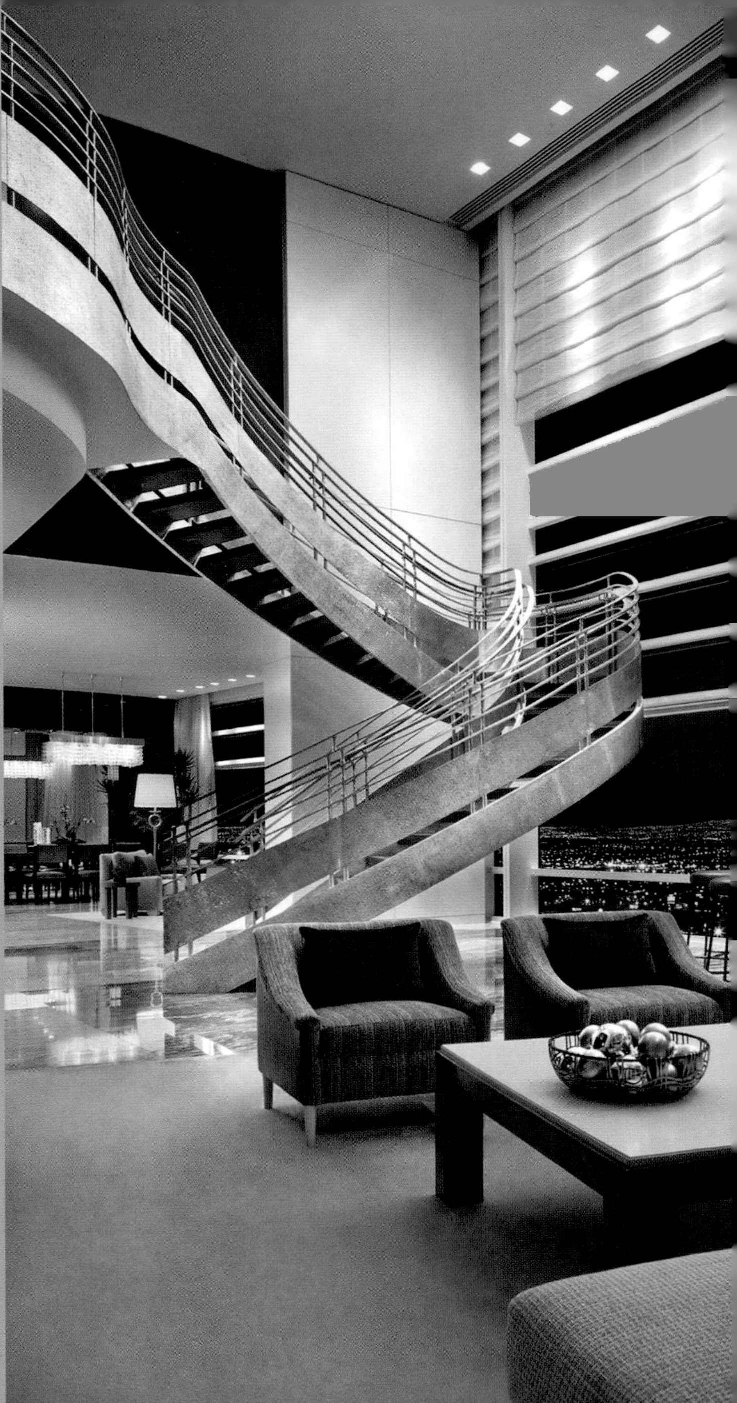

Sleep

Las Vegas has a great range of places to stay, with options to suit all tastes and budgets. In this section, establishments are listed alphabetically.

SLEEP

Introduction

Las Vegas is one of the few cities where you can eat, drink, shop and be entertained without even needing to leave your hotel.

Hotels

For a truly unique experience, stay in one of the theme casino hotels on and around The Strip. These are like no others in the world and give you the added benefit of being right in the heart of the action. An increasing number of smaller, more exclusive hotels are popping up that offer an alternative for those who want time out away from the neon jungle. The north end of The Strip has seen better days in places. A few bastions of the "Golden Era" remain but most have undergone extensive renovations, while others are being torn down to make way for dazzling new resorts. If you want a taste of nostalgia, choose a hotel in historic Downtown, a favorite with millions of visitors.

Motels

Las Vegas boasts dozens of motels near The Strip and Downtown. Rates can be rock-bottom and their rooms are normally the last to get booked up, making them a good bet for finding a last-minute room. Most motels don't have casinos, which also means they are also lacking large crowds. Don't expect much more than standard motel lodgings.

GETTING THE BEST DEAL

For the best deal start looking well in advance: In Las Vegas it really does pay to shop around. Set a budget, know where you would like to stay and in what type of accommodations. Generally, prices are lower during the week but room rates fluctuate according to demand—they can change from day to day. Check to see if the city is staging a major convention before deciding when to go, as accommodations will be in demand, making prices higher. If you do your homework first, it's possible to get a luxury hotel room at a budget price.

From top: Circus Circus, one of the oldest hotels on The Strip; the lobby of The Palazzo; the pool at the Aria

SLEEP

Directory

SOUTH STRIP
Budget
Excalibur
Mid-Range
Luxor
Mandalay Bay
MGM Grand
New York New York
Tahiti Village
Luxury
Four Seasons Las Vegas
NoMad Las Vegas
Park MGM
Walkdorf Astoria

CENTER STRIP
Budget
Fairfield Inn Las Vegas Convention Center
Silver Sevens Hotel & Casino

Mid-Range
Alexis Park
Flamingo Las Vegas
The LINQ Hotel & Casino
Palms Casino Resort
Platinum Hotel
Rio All-Suite Hotel & Casino
Treasure Island (TI)
Luxury
Aria
Bally's Las Vegas
Bellagio
Caesars Palace
The Cosmopolitan of Las Vegas
The Palazzo
The Venetian

NORTH STRIP
Budget
Circus Circus

Lucky Dragon
Royal Resort
Mid-Range
Courtyard Las Vegas Convention Center
Shalimar Hotel
SLS Las Vegas
Luxury
Renaissance Las Vegas Hotel
Wynn Las Vegas

DOWNTOWN
Budget
Main Street Station

FARTHER AFIELD
Budget
Eastside Cannery Casino & Hotel
Hawthorn Suites by Wyndham Las Vegas/Henderson

SLEEP

Sleeping A–Z

PRICES
Prices are approximate and based on a double room for one night.

$$$	over $200
$$	$120–$200
$	under $120

ALEXIS PARK $$
alexispark.com
If you prefer to stay off The Strip (▷ 155, panel), this small all-suite hotel has 495 rooms, including some fantastic two-level suites at a really good price. It's also fairly quiet and family-friendly. Facilities include a hot tub and three pools.

The hotel provides guests with free travel to and from The Strip.
➕ E9 ✉ 375 East Harmon Avenue ☎ 702/796-3300 🚌 108

ARIA $$$
aria.mgmresorts.com
Aria is the flagship hotel of the stunning CityCenter complex (▷ 18–19). The rooms and suites have floor-to-ceiling windows to match the glass-walled tower's smooth lines> Guests can enjoy top-of-the-range gourmet dining and nightlife, get pampered at the spa, and swim in the three pools.
➕ C10 ✉ 3730 Las Vegas Boulevard South ☎ 702/590-7757 🚌 Deuce

BALLY'S LAS VEGAS $$$

caesars.com/ballys-las-vegas

Bally's is the place to come for some "me time." The 2,549 rooms and 265 suites are spacious, with grand sitting areas and opulent bathrooms. There are floodlit tennis courts.

➕ D9 ✉ 3645 Las Vegas Boulevard South ☎ 702/739-4111 🚍 Bally's/Paris 🚍 Deuce

BELLAGIO (▷ 14) $$$

bellagio.mgmresorts.com

This is one of the most beautiful hotels in Vegas, built in the style of a huge Mediterranean villa with lovely gardens. The 3,950 rooms and suites are large and classy, and decorated in modern tones.

➕ C9–D9 ✉ 3600 Las Vegas Boulevard South ☎ 702/693-7111 🚍 Deuce, SDX

CAESARS PALACE (▷ 16) $$$

caesars.com/caesars-palace

Ancient Rome prevails through classical temples, marble columns and every possible excess you can imagine. All 3,348 rooms and suites are luxurious, but even more so in the Octavius and Augustus towers, which have huge whirlpool tubs in the bathrooms.

➕ C8–D9 ✉ 3570 Las Vegas Boulevard South ☎ 702/731-7110 🚍 Flamingo/Caesars Palace 🚍 Deuce

CIRCUS CIRCUS (▷ 66) $

circuscircus.mgmresorts.com

Although it is one of the oldest hotels on The Strip, Circus Circus still provides one of the best value-for-money options for families. It has nearly 3,800 serviceable rooms and suites.

➕ E6 ✉ 2880 Las Vegas Boulevard South ☎ 702/734-0410 🚍 Deuce

THE COSMOPOLITAN OF LAS VEGAS (▷ 20) $$$

cosmopolitanlasvegas.com

The sheer-sided tower of The Cosmopolitan, next door to the happening CityCenter (▷ 18–19),

The Flamingo is a good choice if you want to be close to the action

offers nearly 3,000 rooms, studios and suites, some with balconies (a rarity on The Strip) or kitchenette. Cosmo's central showpiece is an amazing multistory chandelier, concealing three bars.

D9 ⊠ 3708 Las Vegas Boulevard South ☎ 702/698-7000 🚌 Deuce

COURTYARD LAS VEGAS CONVENTION CENTER $$

courtyard.marriott.com
Part of the well-known chain, this business hotel provides 140 better-than-average motel rooms (including 6 suites), plus a fitness center and an outdoor pool. It's near the Las Vegas Convention Center, which has a monorail station, and the Allegiant Stadium.

F7 ⊠ 3275 Paradise Road ☎ 702/791-3600 🚇 Las Vegas Convention Center 🚌 SDX

EASTSIDE CANNERY CASINO & HOTEL $

eastsidecannery.com
Only 7 miles (11km) from the airport and close to The Strip, this is a comfy, good-value option if you're going to Hoover Dam and the Grand Canyon. It has a fitness center and mobility scooter hire.

Off map ⊠ 5255 Boulder Highway ☎ 702/856-5300 🚌 202, BHX

EXCALIBUR $

excalibur.mgmresorts.com
Kids love this medieval castle with its moat and drawbridge. Parents might find it all just a little tacky, but it's probably one of the cheapest hotels on The Strip, and has more than 4,000 rooms and suites.

D10 ⊠ 3850 Las Vegas Boulevard South ☎ 702/597-7777 🚌 Deuce, SDX

STAYING OFF-STRIP

If it's your first trip to Las Vegas, you'll want to stay in the heart of the action on The Strip. But to save money, some visitors stay off The Strip instead. It's easy to travel between Downtown and The Strip by bus (or, more expensively, by taxi), but if you decide to book lodgings anywhere else off The Strip, try to pick a property that offers a complimentary shuttle service for guests.

FAIRFIELD INN LAS VEGAS CONVENTION CENTER $

fairfield.marriott.com
About a mile east of The Strip, this pristine, small hotel has a contemporary design. The 142 rooms are decorated in cheerful hues. Start your day with a complimentary hot breakfast buffet. There's a small outdoor pool and a fitness center.

F8 ⊠ 3850 Paradise Road ☎ 702/791-0899 🚌 108

FLAMINGO LAS VEGAS $$

caesars.com/flamingo-las-vegas
Bugsy Siegel's original 1946 Flamingo was rebuilt by the Hilton group in 1993. There are 3,565 rooms; the executive king rooms are spacious. It also has one of the best pool areas on The Strip.

D9 ⊠ 3555 Las Vegas Boulevard South ☎ 702/733-3111 🚌 Deuce

FOUR SEASONS LAS VEGAS $$$

fourseasons.com/lasvegas
This hotel takes up the top five levels of Mandalay Bay (▷ 156), but retains its own tranquil identity. Rooms and suites are elegantly decorated, and the Mandalay Bay facilities are available to guests.

SLEEP

THE HOTEL EXPERIENCE

The fanciful hotel architecture of Las Vegas means that many people come here for the hotel experience alone. Some hotel guests rarely leave the resort's premises—quite understandable when there's an on-site casino, a choice of superb restaurants, world-class shows and shopping, luxury spas and plenty of other leisure amenities. On the downside, the bigger hotels can suffer from slow service and long lines for checking in and out, though express check-out boxes are often available. You simply drop off your keys and leave, and your credit card is charged. Many hotels now offer express check-out services on in-room TVs as well, and some have added automated check-in machines at reception.

➕ D11 ✉ 3960 Las Vegas Boulevard South ☎ 702/632-5000 🚊 Flamingo/Caesars Palace 🚌 Deuce, SDX

HAWTHORN SUITES BY WYNDHAM LAS VEGAS/HENDERSON $

wyndhamhotels.com
Hawthorn Suites is not too far off the beaten track. It's a good choice for families; the 71 suites are plain but some have kitchenettes and a balcony, and lots of extras. There is an indoor pool and fitness center.
➕ Off map ✉ 910 South Boulder Highway, Henderson ☎ 702/568-7800 🚌 217, BHX, HDX

THE LINQ HOTEL & CASINO $$

caesars.com/linq
Right in the middle of The Strip, this casino hotel (formerly the Quad) has 2,600-plus rooms, all freshly renovated with a modern look. It's steps from the High Roller wheel and LINQ Promenade.
➕ D8–D9 ✉ 3535 Las Vegas Boulevard South ☎ 702/322-0560 🚊 Harrah's/The LINQ 🚌 Deuce

LUCKY DRAGON $

luckydragonlv.com
Opened in 2016, this Chinese-themed hotel holds more than 200 plush rooms with vermilion red accents, as well as Asian restaurants and an octagonal casino where a 1.25-ton glass dragon sculpture hangs suspended over the gaming tables.
➕ E6 ✉ 300 West Sahara Avenue ☎ 702/889-8018 🚌 Deuce, SDX

LUXOR (▷ 30) $$

luxor.mgmresorts.com
The 4,400-room Luxor may have moved away from its original Egyptian theme but you still enter beneath a huge sphinx and are transported to some hotel rooms via an elevator that travels up the slope of the pyramid.
➕ C11–D11 ✉ 3900 Las Vegas Boulevard South ☎ 702/262-4444 🚌 Deuce

MAIN STREET STATION $

mainstreetcasino.com
This characterful hotel has a Victorian theme, with genuine antiques, chandeliers, flickering gas lamps, iron railings and stained-glass windows. It has 406 bright rooms and a brewery.
➕ G2 ✉ 200 North Main Street ☎ 702/387-1896 🚌 SDX

MANDALAY BAY $$

mandalaybay.mgmresorts.com
There is masses of big-city style at the Mandalay Bay. It's the only hotel in Las Vegas with a beach and a gigantic wave pool. There

are 3,200-plus rooms and suites;
even the standard rooms are huge,
and all are light and airy.

➕ C11–D11 ✉ 3950 Las Vegas Boulevard
South ☎ 702/632-7777 🚌 Deuce, SDX

MGM GRAND (▷ 34) $$

mgmgrand.mgmresorts.com
This is pure Hollywood, with
figures of famous stars dotted
around the lobby and huge stills
from classic movies on the walls.
The 5,000-plus rooms offer a
range of options, from the health-
conscious "Stay Well" rooms to
large spacious Strip-view suites.

➕ D10 ✉ 3799 Las Vegas Boulevard
South ☎ 702/891-1111 🚇 MGM Grand
🚌 Deuce, SDX

NEW YORK NEW YORK (▷ 44) $$

newyorknewyork.mgmresorts.com
Staying in this huge mock-up of
the New York City skyline is quite
an experience. The 2,000-plus
rooms and suites are in a sophisticated style, decorated in earth
tones and pastels. Light sleepers
should request a room away
from the Big Apple Coaster that
thunders around outside.

➕ D10 ✉ 3790 Las Vegas Boulevard
South ☎ 702/740-6969 🚇 MGM Grand
🚌 Deuce

NOMAD LAS VEGAS $$$

nomadlasvegas.com
The boutique offering is part of
Park MGM (▷ 158) and has all
the attractions of its big-sister
resort but with a more restful,
European feel. Art and opulence
are key features, with its signature
NoMad restaurant a real pull.

➕ D10 ✉ 3772 Las Vegas Boulevard
South ☎ 833/706-6623 🚌 Deuce

THE PALAZZO $$$

venetian.com/towers/the-palazzo
Palazzo is a magnificent all-suite
sister hotel to The Venetian
(▷ 58–59), with similar Italian-
style decor, and plenty of art.
The superb suites have fantastic
views from higher floors. The pool
deck has two seasonal day clubs
(▷ 67), Azure and Tao Beach,
or you can enjoy a sophisticated
nighttime drink at the Electra
Cocktail Club, entertained by DJs
and customized digital artwork.

➕ D8 ✉ 3355 Las Vegas Boulevard
South ☎ 702/607-7777 🚌 Deuce

PALMS CASINO RESORT $$

palms.com
As the name suggests, expect
plenty of tropical foliage at this
towering hotel. The Palms'
reputation is due mainly to the
clientele attracted to its nighttime
haunts, including the APEX Social
Club, which is located on the 55th
floor. The 700 sleek rooms offer
comfortable accomodations,
while the penthouse villas offer
over-the-top luxury.

➕ A9–B9 ✉ 4321 West Flamingo Road
☎ 702/942-7777 🚌 202

SLEEP

PARK MGM $$$

parkmgm.mgmresorts.com

Previously the Monte Carlo, this has a casino, steakhouse, noodle shop and bodega but is understated by Vegas standards. Right next to the T-Mobile arena, it boasts its own theater, making it a great option for showgoers.

D10 ✉ 3770 Las Vegas Boulevard South ☎ 888/529-4828 🚌 Deuce

PLATINUM HOTEL $$

theplatinumhotel.com

This non-gaming, smoke-free retreat is in urban contemporary style. The 255 enormous one- and two-bedroom suites each have a kitchen, a whirlpool tub and a balcony overlooking The Strip or the mountains. Make use of the soothing spa or indoor and outdoor pools.

E9 ✉ 211 East Flamingo Road ☎ 702/365-5000 🚌 202

RENAISSANCE LAS VEGAS HOTEL $$$

marriott.com

For a retreat from the Vegas clamor and commotion, the Renaissance has cool and confident style without a slot machine in sight. The 578 rooms and suites are richly decorated and have a calming effect. There's also a swimming pool, hot tub, fitness center and an upscale steakhouse restaurant.

F7 ✉ 3400 Paradise Road ☎ 702/784-5700 🚌 108

RIO ALL-SUITE HOTEL & CASINO $$

caesars.com/rio-las-vegas

This lively hotel in an off-Strip location offers great entertainment, a rooftop zip-line and two excellent buffets among its dining options. It has 2,548 huge, comfortable suites, with superb views from the floor-to-ceiling windows. There's free shuttle buses to The Strip for guests.

B8–B9 ✉ 3700 West Flamingo Road ☎ 702/777-7777 🚌 202

ROYAL RESORT $

royalhotelvegas.com

The quiet non-casino Royal Resort is just off The Strip and offers good value for money. It has small but comfortable rooms; those at the front have a private balcony. Other amenities include a restaurant, cocktail bar, outdoor pool and gym.

E7 ✉ 199 Convention Center Drive ☎ 702/735-6117 🚌 Deuce

SHALIMAR HOTEL $$

shalimarhotellasvegas.com

This low-rise motel is in a fair location north of The Strip and closer to Downtown. Some of the 100 rooms look out on the on-site wedding chapel. The motel's Florida Café offers Cuban cuisine.

F4 ✉ 1401 Las Vegas Boulevard South ☎ 702/388-0301 🚌 Deuce

SILVER SEVENS HOTEL & CASINO $

silversevenscasino.com

This budget hotel is a mile from The Strip and close to the airport, to which it offers a shuttle service. Although focused on the casino, it has smartly furnished rooms, a pool, hot tub and a 24-hour café, all at agreeable rates.

F9 ✉ 4100 Paradise Road ☎ 702/733-7000 🚌 108

SLS LAS VEGAS $$

saharalasvegas.com

Flowering from the ashes of the vintage Sahara casino, this luxury hotel brand from LA offers up-to-the-minute styling in its 1,600 rooms and more than a dozen nightspots, boutique shops and restaurants.

🔲 E6–F6 ✉ 2535 Las Vegas Boulevard South ☎ 702/761-7000 🚊 SLS Las Vegas 🚌 Deuce, SDX

TAHITI VILLAGE $$

tahitivillage.com

South of The Strip, this non-gaming resort features 300 one- or two-bedroom suites, equipped with either a full kitchen or kitchenette. Guests have use of a lagoon-style pool and free shuttles to The Strip and Downtown.

🔲 Off map ✉ 7200 Las Vegas Boulevard South ☎ 855/386-4658 🚌 SDX

TREASURE ISLAND (TI) $$

treasureisland.com

This hotel has left behind its *Pirates of the Caribbean* swashbuckling image of the past for a more sophisticated adult take on the high seas. The nearly 3,000 rooms and suites, all renovated in contemporary style, have floor-to-ceiling windows.

🔲 D8 ✉ 3300 Las Vegas Boulevard South ☎ 702/894-7111 🚌 Deuce

THE VENETIAN (▷ 58) $$$

venetian.com

Famous for its Italianate canals and replica of St. Mark's Square, The Venetian has more than 4,000 all-suite rooms. The decor varies, although all have marble bathrooms and fine furnishings. There are also excellent dining and shopping opportunities here and next door at The Palazzo, its sister resort.

🔲 D8 ✉ 3355 Las Vegas Boulevard South ☎ 702/414-1000 🚌 Deuce

WALDORF ASTORIA $$$

waldorfastorialasvegas.com

Formerly the Mandarin Oriental, this stalwart of the American hotel scene prides itself on personal service. There is a spa and a Michelin-starred restaurant, but its star appeal is that it has no casino, a rarity for upscale Vegas hotels.

🔲 D10 ✉ 3452 Las Vegas Boulevard South ☎ 702/590-8888 🚌 Deuce

WYNN LAS VEGAS (▷ 62) $$$

wynnlasvegas.com

Steve Wynn's incredible casino resort is one of the city's most lavish hotels, occupying almost 50 floors. The 2,700-plus rooms are huge, stylish and equipped with every luxury. There is an artificial lake and mountain and an 18-hole golf course.

🔲 D7–E7 ✉ 3131 Las Vegas Boulevard South ☎ 702/770-7000 🚌 Deuce, SDX

SLEEP

159

Need to Know

This section takes you through all the practical aspects of your trip to make it run more smoothly and to give you confidence before you go and while you are there.

Planning Ahead

WHEN TO GO

With so many of its attractions under cover and not dependent on weather conditions, there's no off-season to speak of in Las Vegas. Avoid high summer if you don't like excessively hot weather, unless you plan to stay indoors.

TIME

Vegas is on Pacific Standard Time (GMT −8), advanced one hour between mid-March and November.

TEMPERATURE

JAN	FEB	MAR	APR	MAY	JUN	JUL	AUG	SEP	OCT	NOV	DEC
56°F	62°F	68°F	78°F	88°F	98°F	104°F	102°F	94°F	81°F	66°F	57°F
13°C	17°C	20°C	25°C	31°C	36°C	40°C	39°C	34°C	27°C	19°C	14°C

Summer (June to September) can be incredibly hot and oppressive, with daytime temperatures sometimes soaring as high as 120°F (49°C).

Spring and fall are much more comfortable, with average temperatures better suited to exploring outside attractions.

Winter (December to February) sees average temperatures above 50°F (10°C). There can be the odd chilly or rainy day when you will need a jacket and an umbrella, and sometimes it can drop below freezing at night.

WHAT'S ON

March and September
NASCAR Weekend (mid-Mar): A major event on the racing calendar, held at Las Vegas Motor Speedway.
St. Patrick's Day Parade (Mar 17): A pub crawl Downtown kicks off other entertainment; Celtic bands, storytellers and dancers.

April *Vegas Uncork'd*:
The city's premier food and wine festival brings foodies, chefs and sommeliers to The Strip.

May *Helldorado Days*:
A Downtown parade, rodeo events and country-and-western festival celebrate the city's frontier days.

Billboard Music Awards: Music celebrities gather at the T-Mobile to honor the world's best music.

May/July *World Series of Poker:* The world's best poker players compete for supremacy at the Rio.

July *Fourth of July:* US Independence Day festivities, with general jollity everywhere, including superb fireworks displays at major resorts.

October *Life Is Beautiful Festival:* This annual event celebrates food, music and the arts with big-name acts and celebrity chefs.

November *Rock 'n' Roll Marathon & 1/2:* Wildly costumed runners race past live bands on the neon-lit Strip.

December *National Finals Rodeo* (early Dec): During the 10-day finals, cowboys compete and Las Vegas goes country-mad, dressing up, line-dancing and barbecuing.

New Year's Eve Celebrations: A huge party held along The Strip and Downtown on the Fremont Street Experience.

First Friday A huge arts and entertainment party takes place on the first Friday of each month in Downtown's 18b Arts District (✉ ffflv.org ⏰ 5–11pm).

LAS VEGAS ONLINE
visitlasvegas.com
The official website of Las Vegas Convention and Visitors Authority offers well-presented information on everything you need to know when planning your trip to Las Vegas.

reviewjournal.com
For articles on local news, listings, events and other sources of information, try this useful site run by the respected *Las Vegas Review-Journal*, Nevada's largest newspaper

vegas.com
A comprehensive guide to hotels, entertainment, nightlife, events, attractions, activities and tours; offers online booking.

lasvegasgolf.com
This site has detailed reviews on all the courses open in and around Las Vegas to help you plan a golfing holiday, and decide which courses you want to play.

vegasexperience.com
This lively site is dedicated to the Fremont Street Experience. See what's going on at any time of the year, look for places to stay and find more things to do Downtown.

gaylasvegas.com
A complete site for LGBTQ+ locals and visitors to Las Vegas. It keeps up with the latest information on clubs, bars, restaurants and organizations, plus lots more.

lasvegasweekly.com
A day-by-day guide to events and shows, as well as information on culture, nightlife and eating. It also hosts several podcasts covering what's on in the city.

lasvegas.com
Site offering travel deals and packages on many Las Vegas attractions, including daily discounts on hotels, tickets, museums, rides, helicopter tours and excursions.

USEFUL WEBSITES

rtcsnv.com/transit/
Official site for the Regional Transportation Commission of Southern Nevada (RTC), the company responsible for the Las Vegas bus system. Use the transit system map, routes and schedule pages to discover exactly how to get from A to B.

fodors.com
A complete travel-planning site where you can research prices and weather; book air tickets, cars and rooms; pose questions (and get answers) to fellow visitors; and find links to other sites.

INTERNET ACCESS

Most hotels in Las Vegas have business centers and offer internet access to their guests, but be aware that most hotels charge for internet access (around $10–$20 per day), and for WiFi connection when using your own laptop. It is possible to find free access in some hotels, but usually only if the hotel already charges a mandatory nightly resort fee.

NEED TO KNOW

Getting There

ENTRY REQUIREMENTS

Visitors to the US must show a full passport, valid for at least six months after the period of travel. You must complete an Electronic System of Travel Authorization (ESTA) before traveling to the US. ESTA is a web-based system and valid for two years for stays of up to 90 days (https://esta.cbp.dhs.gov). Most UK citizens and visitors from other countries belonging to the Visa Waiver Program can enter without a visa, but must have a return or onward ticket. Allow extra time for security checks. Regulations can change, so check before you travel with the US Embassy (☎ 020 7499 9000; uk.usembassy.gov).

AIRPORT FACTS

● McCarran airport has two well-organized terminals with many shops, restaurants and snack bars.
● The airport underwent a $500-million expansion, with a new terminal, in 2012.
● 50 million passengers per year pass through the airport.
● It is the 28th busiest airport in the world.
● It is one of a few airports where you can play the slot machines while waiting for your luggage.

AIRPORT

McCarran International Airport (LAS) is served by direct flights from cities right across North America, and there are intercontinental flights from London, Frankfurt and Tokyo. It is worth checking for special deals from airline and flight brokers, in newspapers and on the internet.

FROM MCCARRAN INTERNATIONAL AIRPORT

McCarran airport (tel 702/261-5211, mccarran.com) is 4 miles (6km) southeast of The Strip, at 5757 Wayne Newton Boulevard. Shuttles (including to McCarran Rent-a-Car Center), taxis and limousines pick up outside the terminals, and there are information desks throughout the airport.

Several companies, including Super Shuttle (supershuttle.com), run shuttle buses every 15 minutes from outside the baggage claim area—leave through door exits 7–13—and on Level Zero at Terminal 3. They all cost around $10 to The Strip or Downtown, and normally operate 24 hours. Most stop at all the major hotels and motels. No advance reservation required. Check first, as your resort hotel might offer an airport shuttle. Less expensive are the RTC buses (rtcsnv.com; from $2 one way) from outside the airport terminal: the Westcliff Airport Express (WAX) bus stops at the corner of Tropicana Ave and Las Vegas Blvd, where you can transfer to the Deuce (▷ 166), which stops close to most hotels along The Strip, or the faster Strip & Downtown Express (SDX) bus (▷ 166), which makes limited stops.

Taxis are easily available outside baggage claim at Terminal 1 and Level Zero at Terminal 3, and cost around $25 to the center of The Strip, or $35 to Downtown hotels. Uber and Lyft operate in Vegas and can cost 30 percent less than taxis.

Stretch limos line up outside the airport to take you to your destination if your budget allows (rates vary from $60 up to $115 per hour, depending on the size). Try Presidential Limousines (tel 702-438-5466, presidential-limolv.com). For car rentals, all major car rental companies are located off-site (▷ panel). There are buses and shuttles available to take you to the McCarran Rent-a-Car Center, about 3 miles (5km) from the terminals. It is better to reserve a car in advance.

ARRIVING BY BUS
Greyhound (tel 800/231-2222, greyhound.com) operates services to Las Vegas from cities and towns in California and Nevada. Tickets can be purchased just prior to departure. This is a convenient and inexpensive way to travel, although not the most comfortable. All Greyhound buses arrive at Downtown's bus terminal at 200 South Main Street (tel 702/384-9561).

ARRIVING BY CAR
Interstate 15 from Los Angeles to Vegas takes you through some of the most breathtaking scenery of the Mojave Desert. The journey takes 4–5 hours depending on road, weather and traffic conditions (delays are often caused by construction work). Carry plenty of water and a spare tire, and watch your fuel level.

ARRIVING BY RAIL
Amtrak (tel 800/872-7245, amtrak.com), the national train company, does not offer a direct service to Las Vegas from Los Angeles. You can connect to the city by bus from other rail destinations in California and Arizona.

A long-awaited new high-speed rail line from Los Angeles to Las Vegas is finally due to complete in 2023.

CAR RENTAL

Hotel information desks can advise about renting a car. Some companies will deliver to hotels and pick up at the end of the rental period.

Avis	702-531-1500
Budget	702-736-1212
Enterprise	702-795-8842
Hertz	702-262-7700
National	702-263-8411
Thrifty	702-896-7600

The airport's off-site McCarran Rent-a-Car Center is serviced by all the major rental companies. All customers will be transported to their vehicles by free shuttles. For information, call 702-261-6001.

CUSTOMS

● Visitors from outside the US, aged 21 or over, may import duty-free: 200 cigarettes, or 100 cigars, or 2kg of tobacco; 1 liter of alcohol; and gifts up to $100 in value.
● Imports of wildlife souvenirs sourced from rare or endangered species may be illegal or require a special permit. Check your home country's customs rules.
● Restricted import items include meat, seeds, plants and fruit.
● Some medication bought over the counter abroad may be prescription-only in the US and could be confiscated. Bring a doctor's certificate for essential medication.

Getting Around

If you are a wheelchair user, on arrival at the airport you will find shuttle buses with wheelchair lifts to get you into the city. You will also find easy access to most restaurants, showrooms and lounges. All the hotel casinos have accessible slot machines, and many provide access to table games. Assisted listening devices are widely available. If you plan to rent a car, you can request a temporary disabled parking permit ($8.25–$13.15), which can be used throughout Nevada; contact the Nevada Department of Motor Vehicles (☎ 486-4386, dmvnv.com).

WALKING

The Strip is 4 miles (6km) long, and it's a taxing walk in the heat. Wear comfortable shoes, sunglasses and sunscreen. Even if you use The Strip's transportation, you will still have to walk considerable distances to and from hotels and attractions. Overhead walkways and trams connect several places along The Strip. Make a note of the cross streets that punctuate The Strip to help get your bearings; some are named after the hotels along them.

Most of what you will want to see and do in Las Vegas is found along Las Vegas Boulevard South, which is well served by buses. The boulevard is divided into two parts: Downtown, between Charleston Boulevard and Washington Avenue; and The Strip, comprising several long blocks— Sahara, Spring Mountain, Flamingo and Tropicana avenues. In 2004, the first leg of a multimillion-dollar monorail was launched, providing a welcome addition to the options for getting up and down The Strip.

BUSES

The RTC (Regional Transportation Commission of Southern Nevada (▷ 163), tel 702/228-7433, rtcsnv.com), runs 55 bus routes throughout the entire system, some of which operate 24 hours a day. South Strip Transfer Terminal (SSTT) at Gillespie Street is a major transfer point. The Deuce provides transportation along The Strip between the SSTT and Downtown, with many stops along the way, and runs about every 15 minutes (during peak times), 24 hours a day. This double-decker bus accommodates 97 people. The faster Strip & Downtown Express (SDX) bus follows nearly the same route, making limited stops along Las Vegas Boulevard. The fare is $6 one-way, $8 for a day pass or $20 for a three-day pass, purchased via the RideRTC app, on the bus or from vending machines (you need to have the exact fare). You can get a transfer from the driver for off-Strip destinations, so you don't have to pay again. Off-Strip buses otherwise cost $2 one-way.

DRIVING

Almost every hotel on Las Vegas Boulevard South has its own self-parking garage. The best way into these garages, avoiding the gridlock on The Strip, is via the back entrances. Valet parking is also available at the front (and sometimes other) entrances. The standard tip for valets is $2–$3 when they return your keys. The best advice about driving in Las Vegas is don't do it unless you have to.

The speed limit on The Strip is 30mph (48kph) north of Tropicana Avenue, 45mph (72kph) south of Tropicana Avenue. The wearing of seat belts is compulsory.

MONORAILS

The monorail (tel 702/699-8222, lvmonorail. com) opened in 2004. Running from MGM Grand to SLS, it operates every day from 7am to 2am (Fri–Sun until 3am, Monday until mid-night). It will take you from one end of The Strip to the other in just 15 minutes. There are seven stations: MGM Grand, Bally's/Paris, Flamingo/Caesars, Harrah's/The LINQ, Las Vegas Convention Center, Westgate Las Vegas and SLS Las Vegas. A single fare costs $5, an unlimited one-day pass is $13 and an unlimited three-day pass costs $29, with 10 percent savings if you purchase online. A number of smaller free tram services run courtesy of the hotels, including one between the Bellagio, CityCenter and Park MGM (every 15 minutes, 8am–4am), one between the Mandalay Bay, the Excalibur and the Luxor (every 5–7 minutes, 9am–10.30pm), and one between the Mirage and Treasure Island (every 5–15 minutes, 7am–2am).

TAXIS AND LIMOUSINES

Taxis line up outside every hotel and can be called from your room. When out, you need to call or go to a cab stand; taxis can't be hailed in the street. Taxi drivers are familiar with all the shows and attractions, and can often make recommendations. Remember to give more of a tip than the standard 10–15 percent of the fare. Uber and Lyft are considerably cheaper than standard taxis. Limousine services start at $45 ($60 for a stretch limo) per hour. Your hotel concierge can assist in making the necessary arrangements. Suggested taxi companies:

- ACE Cab Co. 702/888-4888
- Presidential Limousine 702/438-5466
- Western Cab Co. 702/736-8000
- Yellow Checker Star 702/873-8012, ycstrans.com

ORGANIZED SIGHTSEEING

There is no shortage of Vegas-based tour companies offering trips from Vegas to wherever you want to go, but there are also plenty showing the best of the city sights. These tours can give you an insider's view on city attractions, along with a good overview and orientation, before you start exploring independently. Nearly every hotel in Las Vegas has a sightseeing desk from where you can book tours. If the tour bus approach doesn't appeal to you, there are all kinds of other options, including small-scale specialized tours with your own group of family or friends, or using a limousine to whisk you from place to place. Perhaps best of all, you can take to the skies in a helicopter for a bird's-eye view of the fantastic architecture and, on after-dark flights, the glittering lights. Reputable tour companies include Scenic Airlines (scenic.com), Pink Jeep Tours (pinkjeeptours.com) and Maverick Helicopters (maverickhelicopter.com) and Gray Line Tours (graylinelasvegas.com).

Essential Facts

In medical emergencies call ☎ 911 or go to the emergency department of the nearest hospital. Emergency Room services are available 24 hours at University Medical Center (✉ 1800 West Charleston Boulevard ☎ 702/383-2000, umcsn. com), or Sunrise Hospital and Medical Center (✉ 3186 South Maryland Parkway ☎ 702/731-8000, sunrisehospital.com). Pharmacy telephone numbers are listed under "Pharmacies" or "Drugstores" in the Yellow Pages (yellow-pages.com). 24-hour and night pharmacies are available at Walgreens (✉ 3339 Las Vegas Boulevard South ☎ 702/369-8166, walgreens. com), and at CVS (✉ 3758 Las Vegas Boulevard South ☎ 702/262-9284, cvs.com).

ELECTRICITY

Voltage is 110/120 volts AC (60 cycles) and sockets take two-prong, flat-pin plugs or three-pronged plugs with an additional rounded ground. European appliances also need a voltage transformer.

EMERGENCY NUMBERS

Police/fire/ambulance: 911
American Automobile Association (AAA) breakdown service: 800/222-4357.

ETIQUETTE

● Tip staff at least 15–20 percent in a restaurant, taxi drivers 10–15 percent for a direct route, porters $2–$3 per bag, depending on the distance carried, and valet parking attendants $2–$3 when they return your car.

● Las Vegas is one of the most lenient places for smoking in the US. Most hotels have designated smoking rooms, but smoking isn't allowed inside shopping malls, restaurants or bars that serve food. In 2017, recreational marijuana use became legal in Nevada, although restrictions apply.

● Dress is very informal during the day, and shorts and T-shirts are generally accepted anywhere. In the evening, smart-casual is more the norm, and some lounges, nightclubs and restaurants may have a dress code.

GAMING

Nevada law permits a wide variety of gaming, but the most popular games are roulette, blackjack, craps and slot machines. If you are new to the game, spend some time watching before actually taking the plunge; you could pick up a few tips from the hard-and-fast gamblers. Punters have to be 21 to play. Most casinos do not have windows or clocks, so you are unaware of time passing, and they will often keep you refueled with free drinks and snacks. One benefit of all this cash changing hands is that much of the gaming taxes collected by the state are funneled into public education.

Glossary of terms:

Action Gaming activity measured by the amount wagered.

Bank The person covering the bets in any game, usually the casino.

Buy-in Purchasing of chips.

Cage The cashier's section of the casino.

Even money Bet that pays off at one to one.

House edge The mathematical advantage the casino enjoys on every game and wager.

House odds The ratio at which the casino pays off a winning bet.

Limit The minimum/maximum bet accepted.

Loose machine A slot machine set to return a high percentage on the money you put in.

Marker An IOU owed to the casino by someone playing on credit.

Toke A tip or gratuity.

LOST PROPERTY

● For property lost on public transportation: South Strip Transfer Terminal, South Gilespie Street, tel 702/676-1849; daily 6–10.

● For property lost at McCarran International Airport: tel 702/261-5134; daily 7.30–6.

● Report losses of passports or credit cards to the police.

NATIONAL HOLIDAYS

Jan 1: New Year's Day
3rd Mon in Jan: Martin Luther King Jr. Day
3rd Mon in Feb: President's Day
Mar/Apr: Easter (public holiday Good Friday)
Last Mon in May: Memorial Day
Jul 4: Independence Day
1st Mon in Sep: Labor Day
2nd Mon in Oct: Columbus Day
Nov 11: Veterans Day
4th Thu in Nov: Thanksgiving
Dec 25: Christmas Day

OPENING HOURS

● Casinos: 24 hours a day, 7 days a week.

● Banks: Mon–Fri 9–5 or later, and some Sat mornings and early afternoons.

● Post offices: normally Mon–Fri 9–5, with limited hours on Sat.

MONEY

● Credit cards are widely accepted.

● Most banks have ATMs.

● US-dollar traveler's checks are still accepted as cash in most places, but ID will usually be requested.

● Most major hotels will exchange foreign currency, and there are several exchange bureaus on The Strip. You can also change money at major banks.

CURRENCY

The unit of currency is the dollar ($), divided into 100 cents. Bills (notes) are in denominations of $1, $5, $10, $20, $50 and $100. Coins are 1 cent (penny), 5 cents (nickel), 10 cents (dime), 25 cents (quarter) and 50 cents (half dollar).

NEWSPAPERS AND MAGAZINES

● Las Vegas has two daily newspapers: the *Las Vegas Review-Journal* and the *Las Vegas Sun*.
● Free *Las Vegas Weekly* has club listings and restaurant and bar reviews.
● *Las Vegas Magazine* is a free tourist publication containing coupons.

TELEPHONES

US cellphone services are highly affordable and are a good alternative for overseas visitors to their usual phone. Public payphones exist but are becoming scarcer. Some phones are equipped to take prepaid phone cards and/or credit cards. Dial 1 plus the area code for numbers within the United States and Canada (note that international rates apply for the latter). Calls made from hotel rooms are very expensive. Las Vegas's area code is 702, which does not need to be dialed if you are calling within the city. To call Las Vegas from the UK, dial 00 followed by 1 (the code for the US and Canada), then the number. To call the UK from Las Vegas, dial 00 44, then drop the first zero from the area code.

● Stores: usually open at 10am; closing times vary, and may be earlier or later on weekends.
● Museums: see individual entries for details.
● Las Vegas boasts that it never closes and never sleeps, but off-Strip stores and banks, and peripheral businesses, will be closed on Sundays and on certain holidays.

POST OFFICES

● Main post office: 1001 East Sunset Road, near the airport, tel 702/361-9200; Mon–Fri 8–9, Sat 8–4. There are many post offices in the city. You can also mail letters and parcels from your hotel.
● Buy stamps from shops and from machines.
● US mailboxes are blue.

SENSIBLE PRECAUTIONS

Carry only as much money with you as you need; leave other cash and valuables in the hotel safe. At night, avoid hotel parking lots and always enter the hotel via the main entrance. Report theft or mugging on the street to the police department immediately. Make sure your room is locked when you leave. Locks can be changed regularly in hotels for security reasons. Keep a close eye on your chips when playing the casino tables as thefts have been reported.

STUDENT TRAVELERS

Discounts are sometimes available to students who have an International Student Identity Card (ISIC).

TOILETS

There is never a shortage of clean, free public restrooms to be found on The Strip and Downtown in hotels, casinos, restaurants and bars.

TOURIST INFORMATION OFFICE

Las Vegas Visitor Information Center: 3150 Paradise Road, Las Vegas, NV 89109, tel 702/892-7575, visitlasvegas.com, open Mon–Fri 8–5.30.

Books and Films

BOOKS

Fear and Loathing in Las Vegas by Hunter S. Thompson (1971). Hallucinogenic, drug- and alcohol-fueled misadventures of "gonzo" journalist Thompson and his deranged lawyer. Made into a film (1998) starring Johnny Depp.

Inside Las Vegas by Mario Puzo (1977). Illustrated retrospective of vintage Vegas by *The Godfather* author, with grainy photos revealing the seamier side of life on The Strip.

Literary Las Vegas: The Best Writing About America's Most Fabulous City edited by Mike Tronnes (1995). Anthology of essays and short stories about Vegas mobsters, showgirls and atomic bomb testing.

When the Mob Ran Vegas by Steve Fischer (2005). Subtitled "Stories of Money, Mayhem and Murder," it covers the colorful but scary characters who controlled Sin City in the 1950s and 1960s.

Of Rats and Men by John L. Smith (2019). The biography of former mob defense lawyer and ex-Vegas mayor, Oscar Goodman, tells the tale of the city's underbelly as well as his role in its revitalization.

FILMS

Ocean's 11 (1960). Buddies behaving badly, starring Frank Sinatra, Dean Martin and Sammy Davis Jr. as 11 old friends planning to rob five Vegas casinos in one night. The remake trilogy began with *Ocean's Eleven* (2001), followed by *Ocean's Thirteen* (2007) and *Ocean's Eight* (2018).

Rain Man (1988). Conniving Charlie Babbitt (Tom Cruise) tries to dupe his autistic savant brother Raymond (Dustin Hoffman) into hitting the jackpot at Caesars Palace.

Casino (1995). Corrupt casino boss Sam Rothstein (Robert De Niro) looks on as his city transforms from mobster empire to family-friendly resort. A powerful Martin Scorsese epic, soaked in blood, power and greed.

The Hangover (2009). When everything that could go wrong during a stag party in Vegas does, raunchy hijinks ensue.

SIN CITY

With its origins firmly rooted in vice, corruption and scandal, Las Vegas has always provided a rich source of material for novelists and screenwriters. The weird, the shocking and the extreme are everyday occurrences in real life, re-created in gangster thrillers, such as *Casino*; glitz musicals, like *Viva Las Vegas* starring Elvis Presley; and the escapist road-trip fantasy novel and film *Fear and Loathing in Las Vegas*. And as the ultimate dream of many visitors is to be the lucky one to defy the casino's odds and break the bank, Sin City is likely to be a source of inspiration for many years to come.

Index

173

We would like to thank the following photographers, companies and picture libraries for their assistance in the preparation of this book:

2t AA/C Sawyer; 2ct Neon Museum; 2c SlotZilla; 2cb MGM Resorts International; 2b AA/C Sawyer; 3t MGM Resorts International; 3ct Gabriele Stabile; 3cb MGM Resorts International Stock Photo; 4t AA/C Sawyer; 5 SV/Alamy Stock Photo; 6/7t AA/C Sawyer, 6r AA/C Sawyer; 6/7ct AA/C Sawyer; 6/7b Kobby Dagan/VWPics/Alamy Stock Photo; 7l AA/C Sawyer; 8/9t AA/L Dunmire; 8/9ctl Stratosphere Hotel/Marc Paulus; 8/9ctr Harrahs/courtesy of Caesars Palace Las Vegas; 8/9cbl AA/C Sawyer, 8/9cbr MGM Resorts International, 8/9b Caesars Entertainment; 10bl Getty Images; 10br Bloomberg/Getty Images; 11 MGM Resorts International; 12 Neon Museum; 14 AA/C Sawyer; 14/5ct AA/L Dunmire; 14/5cb Mathew Allen; 15 AA/L Dunmire; 16 AA/Sawyer; 17ct, 17cb AA/C Sawyer; 17r Harrahs/courtesy of Caesars Palace Las Vegas; 18l MGM Resorts International; 18tr Jerry Ballard/Alamy Stock Photo; 18/9c Alun Reece/Alamy Stock Photo; 19l eye35.co.uk/Alamy Stock Photo; 19r Shirley Kilpatrick/Alamy Stock Photo; 20l, 20/21 David Giral/Alamy Stock Photo; 22 AA/C Sawyer; 23tl AA/C Sawyer; 23cl Sundlof – EDCO/Alamy Stock Photo; 23r, 24l, 24/25t AA/C Sawyer; 24/5b Robert Harding World Imagery/Alamy Stock Photo; 25, 26l, 27l, 27tr, 27cr AA/C Sawyer; 28 Caesars Entertainment; 28/9t Caesars Entertainment/Denise Truscello; 28/9b Caesars Entertainment/Denise Truscello; 29 FLY LINQ Zipline at The LINQ Promenade; 30 MGM Resorts International; 30/1t AA/L Dunmire; 30/1c, 31t, 31c MGM Resorts International; 32 Madame Tussauds; 32/3t, 32/3b AA/C Sawyer; 33cr Keylime, 36, 37tl, 37tr, MGM Resorts International; 37c Thiago Santos/Alamy; 38/9 The Mob Museum; 39t The Mob Museum/John Gurzinski; 39c The Mob Museum/Jeff Green; 40 Courtesy of the Atomic Testing Museum, Las Vegas, Nevada, atomictestingmuseum.org; 40/1 Jeff Greenberg 6 of 6/Alamy Stock Photo; 42, 42/3, 43 Neon Museum; 44 MGM Resorts International; 44/45t, 45cr, 45tr, 45c, 46l, 46tr, 46/47c, 47tl, 47r AA/C Sawyer; 48tl, 48cl, 48/9 MGM Resorts International; 49cr AA/C Sawyer; 50l AA/L Dunmire; 50/51, 51r, 52, 53tl AA/C Sawyer; 53ct, 53cl, 53cr MGM Resorts International; 54l, 54/55, 55tr, 55br courtesy of The Smith Center; 56l, 56/57t AA/C Sawyer; 56cr Stratosphere Hotel; 57, 58tl, 58/59c, 59tl, 59tr, 59cr, 60, 61r AA/C Sawyer; 60/1t, 60/1b A Little White Chapel; 62l, 62/33t AA/C Sawyer; 62cr John Warburton-Lee Photography/Alamy Stock Photo; 63cl AA/C Sawyer; 63cr Wynn Las Vegas; 64 Slotzilla; 66bl The Auto Collections, Las Vegas; 66br Canyon Ranch; 67bl, 67br, 68bl MGM Resorts International; 68br Gameworks, Las Vegas; 69b, 70 AA/C Sawyer; 71bl Hollywood Cars Museum; 71br PCL/Alamy Stock Photo; 72bl Caesars Entertainment; 72br John Elk III/Alamy Stock Photo; 73bl Pole Position Raceway; 73br Slotzilla; 74bl AA/C Sawyer; 74br MGM Resorts International; 75 Niebrugge Images/Alamy Stock Photo; 76bl Tibor Bognar/Alamy Stock Photo; 76br Photodisc; 77bl, 77br, 78bl, 78br, 79bl, 79br AA/C Sawyer; 80 MGM Resorts International; 82c, 82b AA/C Sawyer; 83t, 83b MGM Resorts International; 86t AA/L Dunmire; 86ct MGM Resorts International; 86cb AA/C Sawyer; 86b Darrin Bush Las Vegas News Bureau, 88t, 88c AA/C Sawyer; 88b MGM Resorts International; 89t AA/C Sawyer; 89b AA/L Dunmire; 92br, 94t, 94b AA/C Sawyer; 95t Yaacov Dagan Alamy Stock Photo; 95b AA/C Sawyer; 98t Stratosphere Hotel; 98c, 98b AA/C Sawyer; 100cl The Mob Museum; 100cr PCL/Alamy Stock Photo; 101t Neon Museum; 101b, 104t, 104ct AA/C Sawyer; 104c The Mob Museum; 104cb Neon Museum; 104b courtesy of The Smith Center; 105 Slotzilla; 106c AA/M Van Vark; 106b, 107t AA/C Sawyer; 107b Getty Images; 110t, 110c, 111, 112, 114/115t, 114ct, 114cb, 114/115b, 115ct, 115cb AA/C Sawyer; 118 Richard Green/Alamy Stock Photo; 120, 123 AA/C Sawyer; 124 MGM Resorts International; 126/127t AA/C Sawyer; 126ct The Wynn/Tomasz & Rossa; 126cb MGM Resorts International, 126/127b, 127ct AA/C Sawyer; 127cb MGM Resorts International; 130 AA/C Sawyer; 133 Penn & Teller; 135 Aurora Photos/Alamy Stock Photo; 136 Gabriele Stabile; 138t ImageState; 138ct MGM Resorts International, 138cb AA/C Sawyer; 138b MGM Resorts International; 145 AA/C Sawyer; 148 Kumar Sriskandan/Alamy Stock Photo; 150 MGM Resorts International; 152t, 152c AA/C Sawyer; 152b MGM Resorts International; 154 AA/C Sawyer; 160 Kumar Sriskandan/Alamy Stock Photo.

Every effort has been made to trace the copyright holders, and we apologize in advance for any unintentional omissions or errors. We would be pleased to apply any corrections in a following edition of this publication.

Las Vegas 25 Best

WRITTEN BY Huw Hennessy, Jackie Staddon and Hilary Weston
UPDATED BY Jane Egginton
SERIES EDITOR Clare Ashton
COVER DESIGN Jessica Gonzalez
DESIGN WORK Liz Baldin
IMAGE RETOUCHING AND REPRO Ian Little

ISBN 978-1-64097-338-1

SEVENTH EDITION

Printed and bound in China by 1010 Printing Group Limited.

10 9 8 7 6 5 4 3 2 1

A05743
Maps in this title produced from map data supplied by Global Mapping, Brackley, UK © Global Mapping and data available from openstreetmap.org © under the Open Database License found at opendatacommons.org
Transport maps © Communicarta Ltd, UK